GOVERNMENT
AND THE
CORPORATION

GOVERNMENT AND THE CORPORATION

Ralph K. Winter

American Enterprise Institute for Public Policy Research
Washington, D.C.

Ralph K. Winter is William K. Townsend Professor of Law at the Yale Law School and an adjunct scholar of the American Enterprise Institute.

Portions of this monograph have been previously published by the Journal of Legal Studies. The author would like to thank the following for reading and commenting on various drafts of this work: Bruce A. Ackerman, John T. Baker, John R. Bolton, Robert H. Bork, Ward S. Bowman, Jr., Marvin A. Chirelstein, Robert C. Clark, Arthur A. Leff, Robert Litan, W. S. Moore.

Library of Congress Cataloging in Publication Data

Winter, Ralph K.   1935-
   Government and the corporation.

   (AEI studies 211)
     1.   Industry and state—United States.   2.   Corporations—United States.   I.   Title.   II.   Series: American Enterprise Institute for Public Policy Research.
HD3616.U47W54   338.7′4′0973   78-12258
ISBN 0-8447-3313-X

AEI studies 211.

Printed in the United States of America

CONTENTS

3

The Social Control of Corporate Power

4

Summary and Conclusion

1

Introduction

Whatever the origins of the corporate form, two opposing views of its relation to society and government have from the beginning shaped the legal structure surrounding corporate activity. These two philosophies are not merely the stuff of an arcane debate over commercial law; in fact, they reflect fundamental differences over the extent to which government should dominate the activities of its citizens.

In one view, use of the corporate form is a privilege accorded by the state. Because incorporation is not possible without the state's permission, the government is ultimately responsible for overseeing the exercise of corporate powers and ensuring that they are employed for ends approved by the state. Corporate acts are in effect acts of government, and corporate managers are accountable to government for their actions.

The counter view is that the corporate form is essentially a matter of contract between private parties. Here the state has no more responsibility or authority than with any other contract. Most if not all of the major attributes of the corporation, including its limitation of liability to the amount of one's investment, are attainable through contract. According to this view, the function of general corporation codes is not to grant a privilege but merely to reduce the transaction costs of private bargaining by providing a code of standard legal arrangements.

Both views have suffered criticism over time. The view that incorporation is a privilege lost much of its influence on corporate law in the nineteenth century amid charges of monopoly and corruption. It was alleged that government authority to grant or withhold charters was being employed to create exclusive franchises—for example, by granting only one corporate charter to operate a steamboat on a given river—and that charters were frequently granted in exchange for political or monetary favors.[1] On the other hand, the view that the corporation is a matter of contract has been charged with leading to the creation of centers of significant power that injure both shareholders and society. Proponents of the "contract" view have thus had to struggle against a movement toward federal intervention to control corporate power.

Proposals for the federal regulation of the governance of corporations[2] reflect the "privilege" view and are generally designed to serve two purposes. Their first function is to subject corporate management to restrictions for the sake of protecting shareholders from the self-dealing of management or from actions with which shareholders may disagree. The second purpose is to regulate the structure and behavior of corporate management so as to alter the relation of firms to society. The legislative devices available to achieve these ends are also twofold. One type of legislation, federal "minimum standards," would subject corporate management to a variety of restrictions. The second legislative device would involve federal chartering of all corporations of a certain size. Charters would condition the very existence of the corporation upon compliance with certain structural and substantive requirements.

Adoption of such proposals would drastically alter a number of elementary legal principles (or understandings about what the law is) which have accompanied the growth of the American economy for over a century. However elementary they may be, these principles bear repeating. First, most corporate charters are the creations of the laws of individual states. Second, incorporation laws are "general" rather than "special," which is to say that the corporate form is available to all who would use it; applications are not subject to individual approval by a bureaucrat or a legislature. Third, the selection

---

[1] Adolph A. Berle, *Historical Inheritance of American Corporations: Social Meaning of Legal Concepts*, vol. 3, *The Powers and Duties of Corporate Management* (New York: N.Y.U. School of Law, 1950), p. 189.

[2] For a summary of early proposals for the federal chartering of corporations, see Edward Robinson, *Federal Incorporation*, Catholic University Studies in Economics, Abstract Series no. 9 (1954), pp. 13–17. Contemporary proposals include William L. Cary, "Federalism and Corporate Law: Reflections upon Delaware," 83 *Yale L. J.* 663 (1974), hereinafter cited as Cary; Joel F. Henning, "Federal Corporate Chartering for Big Business: An Idea Whose Time Has Come?" 21 *De Paul L. Rev.* 915 (1972); Ralph Nader, Mark Green, E. Joel Seligman, "Constitutionalizing the Corporation: The Case for the Federal Chartering of Giant Corporations," hereinafter cited as Nader (subsequently published as *Taming the Giant Corporation* [New York: W. W. Norton, 1976]); Donald E. Schwartz, "Towards New Coporate Goals: Co-existence with Society," 60 *Geo. L. Rev.* 57 (1971); see generally 31 *Bus. Lawyer* (1976).

of a state in which to incorporate is almost always a managerial decision made by the would-be corporation, not dictated by law or administrative decision. Fourth, state corporation law is almost exclusively concerned with the internal governance of the corporation, in particular with the relation of the shareholders to management. Except for federal securities law, this relation is largely subject only to state law. Fifth, most state corporation laws are "enabling" rather than regulatory. That is, they enable private parties to incorporate on terms which they freely choose. Consequently, state laws do not impose extensive restrictions upon the discretion of corporate management, although such restrictions may be written into a corporate charter. Sixth, once incorporated in one state, a corporation generally may do business in any state while continuing to be governed—whether because of constitutional command or judgments about comity between states[3]—by the charter and corporation code of the state of incorporation. Seventh, corporate management is relatively autonomous. Although a wide variety of corporate actions are subject to federal regulations, such as the Sherman Act, the National Labor Relations Act, and occupational safety and health regulations, the structure and mechanisms of corporate governance are for the most part not closely regulated.

This book discusses the issue of corporate managerial autonomy and the role of state and federal law in corporate affairs. It takes up arguments relating to the protection of shareholders and discusses regulating the mechanisms of corporate governance in the name of social control.

---

[3] See S. Kaplan, "Foreign Corporations and Local Corporate Policy," 21 *Vand. L. Rev.* 433 (1968).

2

State Law, Shareholder Protection, and the Theory of the Corporation

The Issues

In the spring of 1977 the Supreme Court rejected a claim that the antifraud provisions of the Securities Exchange Act[1] impose a general fiduciary duty on those who control a corporation to act fairly toward minority interests.[2] By rejecting attempts to expand existing federal authority over internal corporate affairs through interpretation, this decision limited the federal role to preventing fraud in securities transactions. It may well thus increase demands for major federal legislation governing the shareholder-corporation relation. Academic commentators agree almost universally that state corporation codes do not impose sufficiently stringent controls on corporate management and are lax in protecting shareholders. Only federal intervention, they say, can correct this sorry situation. This chapter tests the intellectual foundations of this conventional wisdom against an economic theory of corporate function and control. It concludes that state corporate legal systems do protect shareholders and that state regulation is generally preferable to federal regulation.

Existing federal economic regulation is so pervasive that the absence of federal control over the governance of major economic units seems anomalous to some. But proposals for federal regulation should not, for that reason alone, command automatic acceptance. The Securities Acts are already a substantial exercise of federal responsibility.[3]

---

[1] Securities Exchange Act of 1934, 15 U.S.C. §78 (1970); 17 C.F.R. §240.106–5 (1972).

[2] Santa Fe Industries, Inc. v. Green, 430 U.S. 462 (1977).

[3] Securities Act of 1933, 15 U.S.C. §77a–77aa; Securities Exchange Act of 1934, 15 U.S.C. §78 (1970).

Furthermore, reliance on state codes for internal corporate governance is hardly anomalous. Many vital functions of interstate commerce are governed essentially by state law. Virtually all mechanisms for the transfer of interest in property—whether by will, gift, sale, mortgage, or other secured transaction—are matters of state law. So too are the internal organization of partnerships, joint ventures, and individual proprietorships. It is simply not enough to attempt to justify federal chartering and minimum standards legislation, as some have,[4] on the ground that interstate or international transactions are involved.

When a private transaction imposes no substantial costs on society or third parties, the parties to it should be allowed to arrange their affairs in a way that satisfies them rather than some distant official; they should, in short, be given freedom to "make their own deal." Government intervention should be limited to enforcing private bargains and, where possible, to reducing the costs of bargaining (transaction costs). Government might, for example, reduce these costs by providing a code of standard legal arrangements that makes it easier to bring large numbers of participants together in an economic venture. "Enabling" corporation codes attempt to do precisely that. They are legitimately viewed as a species of the law of contracts rather than a form of economic regulation.[5]

The academic literature calling for a more intrusive federal role in the shareholder-corporation relation makes two basic claims. First, because state corporation codes do not require strict judicial scrutiny of all management activity, they leave shareholders in a vulnerable position. Second, this bias in state corporation law derives from the operation of competitive legal systems. Because corporate chartering can generate substantial revenue for state treasuries, states compete for charters. Since management decides where to incorporate and its interests are adverse to those of shareholders, competition among states engenders a permissive attitude toward management and inadequate protection for shareholders. The vast preponderance of academic opinion, and the conventional wisdom of those, such as Ralph Nader, who chronically favor further contraction of the private sector, is that the federal system works to benefit corporate management at a cost to shareholders. Federal regulation is therefore necessary.[6]

---

[4] Nader, p. 84.

[5] Richard A. Posner, *Economic Analysis of Law*, 2d ed. (Boston: Little, Brown, 1977), pp. 289–96.

[6] See, for example, Cary; Alfred F. Conared, "An Overview of the Laws of Corporations," 71 *Mich. L. Rev.* 623 (1973); Earnest L. Folk III, "Some Reflections of

This chapter is a critical examination of these two propositions of "common knowledge."[7] It tests them against what economics tells us about the functions of, and constraints on, corporate management. It elaborates an economic theory describing the various relations that constitute the business corporation and compares that theory with the legal doctrine which is the culmination of the competition between legal systems for corporate charters. It concludes that (1) competitive legal systems should tend to optimize the shareholder's relation to the corporation, and that (2) state corporation codes seem quite consistent with what economic theory suggests are optimal legal arrangements.

Delaware's "Race for the Bottom" and the Capital Market

Competitive Legal Systems and the Capital Market. No one denies that Delaware's open bidding for corporate charters has steadily lessened the restrictiveness of state corporation law. Restrictions on the longevity of a corporation, the businesses in which it may engage, the issuance of stock, the classes of stock issued, dividend policy, discretion as to the holding of shareholders' meetings, charter amend-

---

a Corporate Law Draftsman," 42 *Conn. Bar J.* 409 (1968); statement of Harvey J. Goldschmid, in *Hearings on Corporate Rights and Responsibilities before the Committee on Commerce of the United States*, 94th Cong., 2d sess. 241 (1976), hereinafter cited as *Corporate Rights*; Richard W. Jennings, "Federalization of Corporation Law: Part Way or All the Way," 31 *Bus. Lawyer* 991 (1976); Stanley A. Kaplan, "Fiduciary Responsibility in the Management of the Corporation," 31 *Bus. Lawyer* 883 (1976); Elvin R. Latty, "Why Are Business Corporation Laws Largely 'Enbaling'?" 50 *Cornell L.Q.* 599 (1965); Nader; *Corporate Rights*, statement of David L. Ratner, p. 383; id., statement of Detlev F. Vagts, p. 332; Donald E. Schwartz, "A Case for the Federal Chartering of Corporation," 31 *Bus. Lawyer* 1125 (1976); "Comment," *Law for Sale: A Study of the Delaware Corporate Law 1967*, 117 *U. Pa. L. Rev.* 861 (1969).

Included in the above are professors teaching corporate law at Columbia, Virginia, Berkeley, Chicago, Cornell, Georgetown, and Harvard. A statement endorsing the general principle of federal intervention on the ground that state law suffers from a "race for the bottom" has been signed by eighty professors from sixty-two law schools. (*Corporate Rights*, pp. 343–46.)

Often cited by advocates of federal regulation is Mr. Justice Brandeis' colorful statement, "Companies were early formed to provide charters for corporations in states where the cost was lowest and the laws least restrictive. The states joined in advertising their wares. The race was one not of diligence but of laxity." Liggett Co. v. Lee, 288 U.S. 517, 558–59 (1933), (dissenting opinion.) Since the "laxity" of which he was complaining lies in the elimination of restrictions on the life of a corporation, total capital, corporate purposes, and the holding of stock in other corporations—all of which we are well rid of—corporate critics have drawn the least obvious conclusion about the social usefulness of the "race of laxity."

[7] Jennings, "Federalization of Corporation Law," p. 991.

ments, the means of electing directors, the sale of assets, mortgaging, and the indemnification of officers are among the restrictions that have been eliminated or diminished by amendments to state corporation codes. The ability of corporations to effect fundamental changes, such as mergers and the elimination of minority shareholders, has increased, as has management's power to work its will in a variety of matters, including some in which it may have a conflict of interest (for example, management compensation).[8]

The history of state corporation law is thus largely a history of the drastic reduction of legal restrictions on management and of the diminishing legal rights of shareholders. This movement has not been random. As corporations have sought charters in states with less restrictive codes, other states have adopted similar codes in response. As a result, the movement toward dwindling restrictions has been national, and the Delaware code is no longer significantly different from those of a number of other states.

The competition among states for charters has thus been an important mechanism generating change in American corporate law. Delaware, where 40 percent of the largest industrial corporations were chartered in 1973,[9] and its competitors candidly admit that the purpose of corporate code revisions has been to attract charters for the significant tax revenues they generate.[10] Delaware has benefited in other ways. Lawyers find that its corporation code makes the state a hospitable jurisdiction in which to litigate issues of corporate law, with the result that the Wilmington Bar enjoys an unusually lucrative practice for a city of Wilmington's size. No one disputes these developments. Rather, the controversy is over their effect on the governance of many of the nation's major economic units.

Although it is avowedly not an original approach, the most celebrated exposition of the conventional academic analysis is "Federalism and Corporate Law: Reflections upon Delaware," by William Cary of the Columbia University Law School, a former chairman of the Securities and Exchange Commission (SEC). Characterizing Delaware as

---

[8] See notes 70–75 below and accompanying text.

[9] Nader, pp. 506–31.

[10] The Delaware legislative revision of the corporation code in 1963 contained a preamble explicitly stating such a purpose (cited in Cary, p. 663). In 1969 the Corporation Law Reform Commission of New Jersey stated: "It is clear that the major protections to investors . . . have come and must continue to come, from Federal legislation. . . . Any attempt to provide such regulations . . . through state incorporation acts . . . would only drive corporations out of the state to more hospitable jurisdictions." (Corporation Law Reform Commission of New Jersey, Report, in *N.J. Stat. Ann.*, tit. 14A, at x-xi [1969]; also cited in Cary, p. 666.)

leading a "movement toward the least common denominator" and a "race for the bottom," Cary argues that Delaware's permissiveness has left shareholders easy prey to self-dealing management. To this unhappy conclusion he adds an attack on the Delaware judiciary and argues that "Gresham's law applies" to its decisions, which "lean toward the status quo and adhere to minimal standards of director responsibility."[11]

Rejecting full federal chartering as "politically unrealistic," Cary calls for federal minimum-standards legislation. He claims this legislation, designed to "raise" the standards of management conduct, would increase public confidence—and investment—in American corporations.[12] This last claim, it is absolutely critical to note, is not that an overriding social goal is sacrificed by state law but that Delaware is preventing *private* parties from optimizing their *private* arrangements.

With all due respect to Cary and to the almost universal academic support for his position, it is implausible on its face. The plausible argument runs in exactly the opposite direction. (1) If Delaware permits corporate management to profit at the expense of shareholders and other states do not, then earnings of Delaware corporations must be less than earnings of comparable corporations chartered in other states; therefore, shares in the Delaware corporations must trade at lower prices. (2) Corporations with lower earnings will be at a disadvantage in raising debt or equity capital. (3) Corporations at a disadvantage in the capital market will be at a disdvantage in the product market, and their share price will decline, thereby increasing chances of a takeover that would replace management. To avoid this result, corporations must seek legal systems more attractive to capital. (4) States desiring corporate charters will thus try to provide legal systems that optimize the shareholder-corporation relation.

The conclusion that Delaware shares must sell for less is implicit in Cary's analysis, for if "higher" legal standards for management conduct would increase investor confidence, investors must have had less confidence in Delaware stocks than in the stocks of other states for more than a generation. This lack of confidence would have long been reflected in the price of Delaware shares. Moreover, any reduction in a corporation's earnings would affect its ability to raise debt capital as well as equity, since the risk of a lender is thereby

---

[11] Cary, pp. 663, 705, 672. The Cary article is so highly regarded that a symposium conducted by the American Bar Association's Committee on Federal Regulation of Securities employed it as a focus for discussion; see 31 *Bus. Lawyer* (1976), especially pp. 863, 883.

[12] Cary, pp. 700, 671–72, 705.

increased and a higher interest rate will be charged. Delaware corporations, therefore, not only face a lower share price but also must pay higher interest rates.

This analysis is not crucially dependent upon the consumers of securities or lenders understanding the intricacies of corporate law or knowing of the general permissiveness of the Delaware code. That, indeed, must be what Cary means when he argues that increased confidence will result from more protective legal systems. A simple comparison of earnings of various corporations, for example, will affect the price of Delaware stocks. Moreover, institutional investors —not to mention investment counselors—cannot be unaware of such crucial facts, and their role in the stock market is so critical that their knowledge alone will sharply affect share price. The claim that Delaware is leading a "race for the bottom" has been made so frequently and by so many that it can hardly be described as a carefully guarded secret. Recent work on the stock market strongly suggests that relatively obscure—even confidential—information is transmitted extremely swiftly and almost automatically affects share price.[13] That the impact of a legal system on investors would be known for over a generation only to law professors and to Ralph Nader is simply not a tenable proposition.

It is not in the interest of Delaware corporate management or the Delaware treasury for corporations chartered there to be at a disadvantage in raising debt or equity capital in relation to corporations chartered in other states. Management must induce investors freely to choose their firm's stock instead of, among other things, stock in companies incorporated in other states or other countries, bonds, bank accounts, certificates of deposit, partnerships (general or limited), individual proprietorships, joint ventures, or present consumption. It is simply not plausible to think that domestic insurance companies seeking profitable investments or Saudi sheiks seeking gainful employment for their petrodollars are at Delaware's mercy. Nor is it plausible to think Delaware corporations raise their capital largely from hapless widows investing their meager inheritances.

As discussed in detail later, a corporation's ability to compete effectively in product markets is related to its ability to raise capital, and management's tenure in office is related to the price of stock.[14] If management is to secure initial capital and have access to capital in the future, it must attract investors away from the almost infinite

---

[13] James H. Lorie and Mary T. Hamilton, *The Stock Market: Theories and Evidence* (New York: Dow Jones–Irwin, 1973), pp. 70–97.

[14] See notes 30–57 below and accompanying text.

variety of competing opportunities. Furthermore, to retain its position, management has a powerful incentive to keep the price of stock high enough to prevent takeovers, a result obtained by making the corporation an attractive investment.

The Cary analysis thus seems implausible a priori because, when unpacked, it appears to be little more than a claim that Delaware can facilitate the monopolization of the capital market, just as it can grant exclusive franchises for taxicabs in Wilmington. But the market for capital is international in scope and involves an undifferentiated product with no transportation costs. Delaware cannot create barriers which prevent capital from flowing to the most attractive investments; any attempt at monopolization will only drive capital from that state.

The fact that other states have found it necessary to change their law in response to Delaware, therefore, strongly suggests that investors do not share Cary's view and in fact believe that they are doing better under Delaware law than under the laws of the other states.

Laxity or Efficiency: The Costs and Benefits of Restricting Management Discretion. The implausibility of the "race for the bottom" argument is obscured because the literature calling for stricter regulation stresses only expected benefits while ignoring costs and is in a real sense the victim of its own rhetoric. To say a legal system is marked by "laxity" implies a cost-benefit judgment about more stringent regulation, but such rhetoric in the shareholder protection area is rarely accompanied by the hard analysis such judgments call for. In truth, a "lax" legal system is neither intuitively nor empirically inferior to a stringent one.

All regulation imposes costs in the way of consumed resources, such as the efforts of accountants or lawyers, which might be put to other uses. When regulations are imposed on private transactions, such as the purchase of a car or investment in a corporation, those transactions are made more costly for all involved. For example, it has been argued that whatever reduction in securities fraud is caused by SEC requirements is offset by the higher costs imposed on securities transactions.[15]

Another way in which regulation imposes costs is in restricting the ability of private parties to arrange their affairs in the way they find most suitable. Often these costs result from well-meaning attempts to protect those parties. Assume, for example, that the quality

---

[15] George J. Stigler, "Public Regulation of the Securities Markets," 37 *Journal of Business* 117 (1964).

of widgets can be determined only by extended use rather than consumer examination. Most consumers purchase widgets on the basis of a company's brand name or on the advice of a local merchant, both of whom find it in their economic interest to maintain a good business reputation. Other consumers, however, purchase low-quality widgets (at the high-quality price) from manufacturers hoping to make a quick profit even at the cost of a bad reputation in the long run. Regulation designed to protect such consumers may operate by general rules applicable to all transactions, not just those the government seeks to prevent. For example, government testing of widgets would apply to all widgets, not just those of low quality, and would thus impose costs on (and thereby reduce in number) the beneficial transactions in high-quality widgets. Regulation may deter blameless conduct as well as that which is conceded to have no social value,[16] and those who call for regulation make an incomplete argument when they take account only of anticipated benefits.

Intervention in private transactions that impose no social cost can be justified only as a means of reducing the costs to the private parties. Thus, a prime function of state corporation codes is to supply standard

---

[16] Other areas provide numerous cases where regulation deters the beneficial along with the detrimental. Because the fear of large defamation judgments may deter the media from printing important but not fully confirmed stories, the First Amendment permits defamation of public officials in the absence of clear and convincing evidence of knowing falsity. This is so even though society gains little from false speech. As Mr. Justice Brennan said in New York Times v. Sullivan, 375 U.S. 254, 279 (1964):

> Allowance of the defense of truth, with the burden of proving it on the defendant, does not mean that only false speech will be deterred . . . [U]nder such a rule, would-be critics of official conduct may be deterred from voicing their criticism, even though it is believed to be true and even though it is in fact true, because of doubt whether it can be proved in court or fear of the expense of having to do so.

Rigorous drug regulation impedes the introduction of beneficial as well as harmful drugs and thus harms those who would benefit from an earlier introduction (Sam Peltzman, *Regulation of Pharmaceutical Innovation* [Washington, D.C.: American Enterprise Institute, 1974]). The foreclosure of advocacy in advertising will increase accuracy but also reduce the incentive to advertise and thus deprive the public of the benefits it would otherwise receive in the form of greater information and increased competition (see Ralph K. Winter, Jr., "Advertising and Legal Theory," in *Issues in Advertising*, David G. Tuerck, ed. [Washington, D.C.: American Enterprise Institute, 1978]). Much of the literature that attacks the performance of the private sector ignores these trade-offs and the high price an imperfect universe exacts for the elimination of *all* pollution, *all* defective products, and *all* fraud. Consumer advocates, for example, routinely ignore the higher costs that fall upon consumers as a result of requiring a variety of safety devices on cars or compelling businesses to comply with a myriad of administrative requests for information (Ralph K. Winter, Jr., *The Consumer Advocate versus the Consumer* [Washington, D.C.: American Enterprise Institute, 1972]).

terms that reduce the transaction costs, and thereby increase the benefits, of investing by eliminating costly bargaining which might otherwise accompany many routine corporate dealings. But substituting a mandatory legal rule for bargaining also may impose a cost by eliminating alternatives which the parties might prefer.

Much of the legal literature calling for further federal regulation either assumes that no costs will fall upon shareholders or undertakes only a cursory "eyeballing" of the potential costs. To be sure, self-dealing and fraud exist in corporate affairs and their elimination is desirable. But at some point the exercise of control by general rules of law may impose costs on investors which damage them in both quantity and quality quite as much as self-dealing or fraud. A paradox thus results: Maximizing the yield to investors generally may— indeed almost surely will—result in a number of cases of fraud or self-dealing; and eliminating all fraud or self-dealing may decrease the yield to shareholders generally.

For example, numerous proposals have been made to increase the power of shareholders over the corporate destiny by enabling them to initiate proposals to be submitted to shareholders, by requiring cumulative voting, by compelling management to make extensive information available to any requesting shareholder, by requiring shareholder votes on certain matters, and so on.[17] There is, however, no established or even apparent connection between increasing shareholder power and increasing the yield to investors. To be sure, the lack of shareholder control may have led to some self-dealing, but the elimination of self-dealing by increasing that control involves a trade-off with corporate efficiency and may well reduce the return to shareholders generally. Whether the amount saved in eliminating isolated instances of self-dealing through increased shareholder control is greater than a general loss in corporate efficiency is the issue, and it is neither intuitively nor empirically self-evident that the Delaware code is not a satisfactory resolution.

Similarly, Cary has criticized the Delaware courts for too readily ratifying management conduct and for not applying a standard of "fairness" to its actions. Even if his description of Delaware law is accurate—and that is not without some considerable doubt—his analysis provides no solution.[18] No one is against "fairness" in the treatment of shareholders. The issue to be addressed is the criteria

---

[17] See, for example, Nader, pp. 201–8, 226–27.

[18] The accuracy of Cary's description of Delaware law has been vigorously challenged by Samuel Arsht, "Reply to Professor Cary," 31 *Bus. Lawyer* 1113 (1976); see also notes 58–61 below and accompanying text.

by which the fairness or unfairness of acts are to be determined. Except perhaps for the implication that whatever the Delaware Supreme Court does is unfair, Cary sets out no relevant criteria.[19] One case that Cary attacks, *Sinclair Oil Corp.* v. *Levien*,[20] for instance, involved a parent corporation which held 97 percent of the stock of a subsidiary and which decided to contract the subsidiary's activities by paying out dividends far in excess of earnings. Although other firms held by the parent were expanding at the time, no corporate opportunities were lost to the subsidiary in question, and the dividends were on a pro rata basis.

Cary would create a rule, based on "traditional concepts of fairness," prohibiting a parent from contracting the operations of a subsidiary during a period of expansion when there are minority stockholders.[21] Consider how deeply such a rule intrudes on a corporation's power to make business decisions. Among the matters which become irrelevant are estimates of the subsidiary's likely success in expansion and the value of competing investment opportunities. No weight whatsoever is given to the much greater risk in those respects taken by a 97 percent holder than by a 3 percent holder. Nor is there any way of preventing the 3 percent holder from blackmailing the 97 percent with the threat of preventing the latter from pursuing the more valuable opportunities. In effect, Cary would give the 3 percent holder a veto on these matters, a rule which cannot plausibly be in the interests of shareholders generally.

Another example involves the standard of care required of directors. Here the Delaware decision attacked by Cary held that directors might rely on summaries, reports, and corporate records as evidence

---

[19] See text accompanying note 11 above. See also Cary, pp. 690–92, where the author examines the composition of the Delaware Supreme Court in recent years. Much is made of the fact that "[a] majority of the justices practiced law in the firms which represent the important corporations registered in Delaware. . ." (p. 691), and that "all but two of the justices have been directly involved in major political positions. . ." such as governor and attorney general (p. 692). The first point is neither surprising nor revealing, but it is true only if one counts a lawyer who, when appointed to the bench, had a general practice in a rural town in southern Delaware as being among those representing "the important corporations registered in Delaware." Cary's second point hardly deserves notice, except perhaps to suggest that he should be envied for having been sheltered from the reality of how one becomes a judge. In fact, the Wilmington bar never controlled the Delaware courts during the period studied. Because the two rural counties dominated the Delaware legislature until reapportionment, political conditions necessitated the judicial appointment of many rural lawyers.

[20] Del. Supp. 280 A.2d 717 (Del. 1971).

[21] Cary, p. 680.

that no antitrust violations were being committed by the company, even though nineteen years earlier the Federal Trade Commission had issued a cease-and-desist order against price fixing.[22] Cary's suggestion is that an internal control system to prevent repeated antitrust violations would have prevented the fines and treble damages paid by the company. The issue, however, is not whether damages might be avoided but whether, even employing a simple negligence calculus,[23] the expected value of damages (probability times likely amount) is greater than the cost of avoiding them. Requiring perfect fail-safe systems in every corporation can be far more costly than any potential loss to shareholders, and Cary presents an incomplete analysis in concluding that loss could have been avoided. He is on more solid ground in suggesting that the need for preventive measures was greater in the particular case in light of past conduct since that is relevant to the likelihood of loss.

The point is not that Cary's position is the "wrong" rule. Rather, it is that interventionist legal rules may reduce the yield to shareholders generally and this cost must be weighed against the benefits to be gained by the reduction of self-dealing or mismanagement. Only by ignoring the cost side of the cost-benefit judgment can one assume that "laxity" always injures shareholders and thus sustain the conclusion that the competition among states for chartering has worked to their detriment.

What rules of law optimally protect shareholders is not self-evident except at ends of the spectrum. For example, proposals to increase shareholder "power" which aid only tiny groups of shareholders or forces outside the corporation to influence corporate behavior through obstruction will not protect shareholders generally. And proposals for extensive judicial scrutiny of business decisions on behalf of 3 percent shareholders would entail rigid rules restricting management's ability to make business judgments. Between these extremes, however, lie a vast number of cases in which the cost-benefit judgment seems inconclusive and the proper role of law unclear. That role can be determined only after an excursion into the question of the extent to which economic considerations discipline the behavior of corporate management.

---

[22] Graham v. Allis-Chalmers Manufacturing Co., 41 Del. Ch. 78, 188 A.2d 125 (Sup. Ct. 1963).

[23] The calculus invokes weighing the probability of harm, the gravity of the resultant injury, and the cost of avoiding it. United States v. Carroll Towing Co., 159 F.2d 169 (2d Cir., 1947), opinion of L. Hand, C.J.

The Theory of the Corporation: Product Competition, the Market for Management Control, and Management Discretion

Do Corporations Live by Law Alone? With a few exceptions, the legal literature is single-mindedly concerned with the discretion corporate management can exercise as a result of the "separation of ownership and control" popularized by Berle and Means.[24] This phrase is no more than a description of the fact that the legal controls on management behavior—such as shareholder voting, derivative suits, the elections of directors—seem unsatisfactory methods of exerting control over corporate affairs.

And so they are when viewed in isolation, but the structure of a legal system does not necessarily reflect the realities of the institutions it governs. A literal student of the Constitution might well be appalled that voters in presidential elections are not even told the names of the people they are voting for (the electors). He might then conclude that there is a "separation of voting and control" in presidential elections and call for strengthening the electoral college. Of course, we all know that a party system unsanctioned by the Constitution transformed the electoral college into an institution with no functional resemblance to the legal system which surrounds it. So, too, can an obsession with the formal legal system surrounding corporations obscure actual functional relations.

The separation of ownership and control is a problem only if corporation law is viewed as a comprehensive, functional description of corporate governance. From another perspective, however, the separation is no more than a routine and sensible division of labor. As Richard Posner has written:

> The [management] group consists of people who are experienced in the business and involved in it on a full-time, day-to-day basis. In contrast, the typical shareholder . . . is not knowledgeable about the business of the firm, does not derive an important part of his livelihood from it, and neither expects nor has an incentive to participate in the management of the firm. He is a passive investor and, because of the liquidity of his interest, has only a casual, and frequently quite brief, relationship with the firm. His interest, like that of a creditor, is a financial rather than managerial interest. . . .
>
> It is no more anomalous that shareholders do not manage or control "their" corporation than that bondholders do

---

[24] Adolf A. Berle and Gardiner C. Means, *The Modern Corporation and Private Property*, rev. ed. (New York: Harcourt Brace Jovanovich, 1968).

not manage or control the corporations whose bonds they hold, or trust beneficiaries the trustee. All three groups have an investment interest.[25]

Similarly, many writers on the subject have criticized the role played by institutional investors in controlling corporate behavior.[26] For the most part, these investors have not attempted to influence management behavior by invoking their rights as shareholders; they find their remedy in the stock market.[27] The criticism, a striking demonstration of the depths of the corporate critics' misunderstanding, is directed at a nonproblem. If a pension fund, for example, were to exert direct control over the firms in which it owned stock, it would have to hire extra managerial personnel to keep informed about the activities of each firm. This undertaking would impose enormous additional salary costs upon the fund, and the increased marginal cost of buying new stock would compel the fund to diminish diversification. And for all this, what would be gained? The fund's managerial personnel would probably be no better qualified than those in the corporations, and their additional "control" would be unlikely to add much in the way of financial return to the pension fund.

The fact that shareholders generally, and major institutional investors in particular, find little need for control strongly suggests that factors other than the formal legal structure profoundly shape corporate performance and provide substantial protection for shareholders. If the law of corporate governance is to make sense, it must take into account the constraints imposed on the parties to corporate transactions. These constraints arise largely from competition in two markets which interact with each other and with the capital market: (1) the market for products and services, and (2) the market for management control.

The Market for Products and Services. The market for products and services in which a corporation competes has three dimensions. The first is defined by the range of goods or services which are reasonably substitutable for those offered by the corporation. The second is geographic and defined by the area in which the goods and services offered by the corporation reasonably compete with those offered by others. The third is temporal and defined by the time it takes

---

[25] Posner, *Economic Analysis of Law*, p. 301.

[26] For example, see Nader, pp. 111–14; Donald E. Schwartz, "Towards New Corporate Goals: Co-existence with Society," 60 *Geo. L. Rev.* 57 (1971), pp. 66–75.

[27] See 5 Securities Exchange Commission, Institutional Investor Study Report, H.R. Doc. no. 92–64, 92 Cong., 1st sess., 2529–2949 (1971).

reasonably substitutable products to enter the market after a price change.

This market is an obvious constraint on corporate management. Virtually all the criticism of state corporation codes assumes success in the product market, for it is that success which creates the alleged opportunity for corporate management to profit at the expense of shareholders. This constraint exists, moreover, whether or not management maximizes profit on behalf of itself. The management that chooses inefficient growth, extravagant expenses in the name of corporate social responsibility, or questionable conduct which leads to civil penalties against the corporation will only reduce the share it might have appropriated directly for itself. As demonstrated in the next section, a drop in share price endangers management.[28] Since shareholders do not distinguish among the causes of reductions in yield to them—whether larceny, high management compensation, civil penalties, inefficient growth for prestige purposes, or "socially responsible" expenditures—success in the product market is a precondition to management's enriching itself or to indulging in non-profit activities.[29] Whether management maximizes the return to itself or adopts other goals does not, in short, affect the share available to shareholders. Management discretion in either case thus depends upon success in the product market.

The Market for Management Control. The obsession with "control" by exercise of legal right has been the cause of neglect of a small but important part of the legal literature and of important economic constraints on corporate management. Henry Manne has written a series of articles arguing that share price and the capital market exert discipline on the behavior of corporate management.[30] The body of his work has yet to be seriously confronted by corporate critics, much less weakened. And while Manne stands out in the legal literature, many economists of varying stripe accept the same propositions as true or at least plausible theories of corporate behavior. William Baumol has written:

---

[28] See below, notes 30–34 and accompanying text.

[29] See Henry G. Manne and Henry C. Wallich, *The Modern Corporation and Social Responsibility* (Washington, D.C.: American Enterprise Institute, 1972).

[30] See Henry G. Manne, "Cash Tender Offers for Shares—A Reply to Chairman Cohen," 1967 *Duke L.J.* 231 (1967); "Our Two Corporation Systems: Law and Economics," 53 *Va. L. Rev.* 259 (1967); "Mergers and the Market for Corporate Control," 73 *J. Pol. Econ.* 110 (1965); "Some Theoretical Aspects of Share Voting," 64 *Col. L. Rev.* 1427 (1964).

Reports of the deliberations of the top levels of management in major American corporations seem to indicate a widespread concern with the performance of the companies' securities. Even in companies which have long refrained from the issue of new stocks and which apparently have no plans for such an issue in the foreseeable future there seems to be a heavy preoccupation with the market's evaluation of the corporation's shares. Whatever the reasons . . . this concern is by itself sufficient to empower the market to oversee the behavior of management. If the businessman is motivated to avoid reductions in the price of his firm's securities and if, in fact, he hopes that those prices will rise rather steadily and dependably with the passage of time, he will be driven to adapt his decisions to this purpose. Behavior which depresses security prices will then conflict with company objectives.[31]

A recent example of this influence on management behavior involves the *Washington Post*, which, soon after going public, abandoned a pliable attitude in collective bargaining and won a brutal labor dispute. Much of the change in the *Post*'s attitude resulted from its going public. The *Post* itself thus reported:

The combination of reduced profits and a public market for the company's stock caused a radical change in the corporate atmosphere at The Post. To satisfy investors, Post executives had to improve their balance sheets. Yet the costs of labor and newsprint were climbing steadily, and a sluggish economy was producing less advertising, and thus less revenue.

Today, at the firm's highest levels, there are still disagreements over the decision to go public. Some think it was a mistake, one which made the company—at least to some extent—a hostage to the stock market. Mrs. Graham and others disagree, arguing that the existence of a market in Post stock only forces management to perform according to standards it should have adopted anyway.[32]

Corporate management's attention to the price of the firm's stock is perfectly understandable, as Manne and others have demonstrated.[33]

---

[31] William J. Baumol, *The Stock Market and Economic Efficiency* (New York: Fordham University Press, 1965), pp. 79–80.

[32] *Washington Post*, February 29, 1976, p. G-1.

[33] Manne, "Our Two Corporation Systems," pp. 265–66: "The management that too freely sacrifices profit for growth will find that the stock market puts a relatively low valuation on its assets. This may offer an aggressive management elsewhere a tempting opportunity to acquire assets cheap, and the result may be

The lower the share price, the easier it is for others to take over the corporation and hire new management. If a firm is mismanaged, robbed, or overly attentive to nonprofit goals, the price of its shares will drop and others will perceive an opportunity to take over the corporation and install new and more efficient management to raise the share price.[34] The takeover may be by way of a proxy fight, purchase of control, or merger. Those who take over the corporation may profit from the compensation received as successful managers or from capital gains generated by the increase in share price that greater earnings allow. Trading in corporate shares, therefore, involves not only the market for capital but also the market for management control. Because the market for management control is related to the behavior of the market for capital, it constitutes a substantial constraint on management conduct.

The implications of these facts for the debate over corporate governance are profound. Product-market competition alone is a pressure on management to maximize corporate profit because pursuit of nonprofit goals will be reflected in the company's earnings and in the price of its stock. Management thus has substantial incentive to maximize profits, an incentive directly related to investor behavior.

Imperfections in the Market for Management Control: Lack of Product Competition. Oliver Williamson has argued that the constraints on management may not be very severe if product-market competition is lacking.[35] Where such competition is limited by government regulation, management may have considerable discretion not to maximize the corporation's profits.[36] Regulation may induce firms not to show "excessive" profits so that price increases will not be denied or more onerous regulation imposed. Thus, additions to the costs of doing business such as lavish community-affairs programs, expensive office furnishings, and high management compensation may not incur the penalties imposed by rigorous market competition.

a merger offer or a takeover bid, a definite threat to the autonomy of the management taken over." See also Robert M. Solow, "The New Industrial State or Son of Affluence," *The Public Interest* (Fall 1967), pp. 102, 107.

[34] The relation of earnings and share price is explored in William J. Baumol, "Performance of the Firm and Performance of Its Stocks," in *Economic Policy and the Regulation of Corporate Securities*, Henry G. Manne, ed. (Washington, D.C.: American Enterprise Institute, 1969), p. 127.

[35] Oliver E. Williamson, "Corporate Control and the Theory of the Firm," in *Economic Policy and the Regulation of Corporate Securities*, pp. 281, 294–95.

[36] See Armen A. Alchian and Reuben A. Kessel, "Competition, Monopoly, and the Pursuit of Money," in *Aspects of Labor Economics*, National Bureau of Economic Research Series (New York: Arno, 1975).

Where legal restraints on competition do not exist, however, the market for management control continues to act as a constraint. For example, where competition is lacking because of an oligopolistic market structure—and here I assume for the sake of the argument that such structures in fact reduce competition—management's incentive to maximize the corporation's earnings is not reduced. Oligopolies—and price-fixing cartels, for that matter—are said to rely heavily on a mutual forbearance among firms, induced by the belief that any price cuts would be matched immediately by competitors. If four firms hold 35 percent, 30 percent, 20 percent, and 15 percent of a market respectively, a price cut by any one would be met by the others, and all would retain the same market share but at a lower price. There is no incentive on anyone's part to bring about such a result.[37] Similarly, a cartel of price-fixers must reach a compromise price that offers a higher return to each member; it must avoid a situation in which all compete.

In either case, however, the price level is determined by a structure of relative costs and assets. Changes in this structure create incentives among firms to cut prices and put pressure on corporate management, whether in an oligopoly or in a cartel, to maximize corporate profits. For example, if one firm increased its costs by lavish contributions to Yale, extravagant office suites, or just plain robbery, its competitors would no longer view a price cut as a fruitless endeavor because the first firm's ability to meet the cut would be impaired. The first firm's earnings would have declined relative to its competitors, and the resultant decline in share price would limit its ability to raise capital either by equity or by debt, since the two markets are related and a decline in share price would mean an increase in interest rate.[38]

Unlike management in a firm protected by law from competition, therefore, management of oligopolistic firms or firms in cartels unprotected by regulatory agencies are under considerable pressure to maximize profit on behalf of the corporation (rather than to divert earnings to themselves) so that stock prices will be high.

Imperfections in the Market for Management Control: Costs of Takeovers. The costs of corporate takeovers determine the effectiveness of

---

[37]There is considerable doubt whether this is a plausible theory. See Richard A. Posner, *Antitrust Cases, Economic Notes, and Other Materials* (St. Paul, Minn.: West Publishing Co., 1974), pp. 118–27.

[38] The relation of share price and interest rate is discussed in Victor Brudney and Marvin A. Chirelstein, *Corporate Finance, Cases and Materials* (Mineola, N.Y.: Foundation Press, 1972), pp. 387–95.

the market constraints described above. If these costs are invariably large, as some have argued,[39] then even larger rewards must be anticipated by those seeking to oust management, and the constraints imposed on the exercise of management discretion may seem relatively weak. The costs of takeovers may be said for our purposes to include four components: (1) requirements of state law, (2) requirements of federal law, (3) management efficiency, and (4) transaction costs.

State law and takeover costs. With the increasing use of tender offers over the last decade has come an increase in the number of state takeover statutes.[40] These laws usually provide that the offeror file certain information with state securities officials a specified time before the offer becomes effective.[41] They further require that the offer, once effective, be kept open for another specified period. Most require that the purchase be on a pro rata basis if less than all the tendered shares are purchased. Some of these laws permit state officials to hold hearings on whether the disclosure is adequate and the offer fair. Others make such hearings mandatory at the request of the target company. Unlike most corporate code provisions, takeover statutes have an extraterritorial effect. They apply not only to companies chartered in the state but also to firms with substantial business contacts with the state, no matter where the stockholders reside.[42]

Although the enactment of takeover laws is usually in the name of shareholder protection and to some extent may further that end, the effect is to make takeovers more difficult.[43] The cost of takeovers is usually increased while the expected gain is correspondingly diminished. The offeror is denied both secrecy and speed while management has a number of legal and nonlegal weapons it can utilize defensively in the meantime, such as "defensive" mergers, the creation of a new class of stock, changes in the procedure for electing or eliminating directors, or an antitrust action. Where hearings are mandatory

---

[39] Williamson, "Corporate Control and the Theory of the Firm," pp. 309–17.

[40] A tender offer is "a public offer to purchase a part of a corporation's stock at a fixed price" (Arthur Fleischer and Robert H. Mundheim, "Corporate Acquisition by Tender Offer," 115 *U. Pa. L. Rev.* 317 [1967]). For an example of a takeover statute, see *Del. Code Ann.*, tit. 8 §203 (West 1953).

[41] For a fuller discussion of these laws and detailed citations, see Donald C. Langevoort, "State Tender-Offer Legislation: Interests, Effects, and Political Competency," 62 *Corn. L. Rev.* 213 (1977); Diane S. Wilner and Craig A. Landy, "The Tender Trap: State Takeover Statutes and Their Constitutionality," 45 *Fordham L. Rev.* 1 (1976).

[42] Langevoort, "State Tender-Offer Legislation," pp. 219–23.

[43] Ibid., pp. 216–40; Wilner and Landy, "The Tender Trap," pp. 9–15; Manne, "Cash Tender Offers."

and the delay is inevitably extended, the conclusion that such statutes are designed to protect incumbent management is inexorable.

Federal law and takeover costs. Another cause of high takeover costs is present federal regulatory law. The antitrust laws, for example, forbid mergers of all but those firms with tiny market shares.[44]

The Williams Act[45] imposes disclosure requirements on persons seeking to purchase substantial amounts of a firm's shares, requires that tender offers be left open for seven days, forbids increases in the tender offer price without compensation to previous sellers, and prohibits offers to purchase stock up to a certain percentage only in order of receipt. All these provisions, like many of the state laws, give management time to fight back and drive up the price of the stock and the cost of takeover, although some argue that the protection offered shareholders results in a net benefit to them.[46] It has been convincingly argued that the federal rules governing proxy fights aid management.[47]

Management efficiency and takeover costs. A high takeover cost may also reflect an efficient management since the cost of a takeover —whether by merger, tender offer or proxy fight—will be closely related to the price of the stock. For the most part, the best-run firm in an industry will have the highest takeover cost in that industry. The higher the ratio of the target firm's stock to the maximum attainable price under perfect management, the smaller will be the expected profits of takeover and the weaker the incentive of existing shareholders to tender their shares. The high cost here differs from others, however, in that a benefit to shareholders is clear. So far as the market for management control is concerned, that kind of high takeover cost is exactly what is called for, because it steers competitors in the market for management control (not the capital market) to the less well-run firms. (Takeovers of course may have purposes other than improving management, such as productive integration.)

Transaction costs of takeovers. The transaction costs of takeovers usually vary with the method used. Some costs, however, must be borne no matter how the takeover is attempted. The most important of these costs is that of acquiring information about firms that would be likely prospects for substantial capital gains if given a more efficient management. In some cases, those who control firms may be

---

[44] Brown Shoe Co. v. United States, 370 U.S. 294 (1962).

[45] 15 U.S.C. §§78m(d), (e), 78n(d)-(f) (1970).

[46] See note 43 above.

[47] See Manne, "Mergers and the Market for Corporate Control," pp. 114–15.

able to make relatively accurate assessments of other firms in the same industry. Suppliers and customers of a firm may also occasionally have information not generally available. But even in these cases information is not easy to obtain. The market for management control is not structured well enough to produce relevant information systematically—not to mention the obstacles to information-gathering created by state and federal laws. The lack of information thus results in a substantial transaction cost.

Other costs depend on the takeover method employed. Mergers entail taking over the entire firm, rather than just a controlling bloc of stock, and they are usually accompanied by some kind of extra payment to management (such as consultant contracts) so that it will consent to the consolidation. In other ways, mergers are cheaper than tender offers and proxy fights.[48] Shares can be exchanged instead of cash, and vertical and horizontal mergers may involve such parties as competitors, suppliers, and customers who have low information costs. Present antitrust policy thus substantially increases transaction costs in the market for management control.

The tender-offer method is cheaper only in that less than 100 percent of the stock need be purchased. Costs include compliance with state and federal law, communication with shareholders and brokers, litigation, and so on.[49] Proxy fights are probably the most expensive method since they include these costs plus additional publicity and propaganda expenses.[50]

Imperfections in the Market for Management Control and Management Discretion. The conclusion that federal regulation is necessary because of imperfections in the market for management control as a result of high takeover costs cannot be quickly drawn. A major portion of these costs may in fact be attributable to the Williams Act's disincentives for tender offers and to a fundamentally wrongheaded antitrust policy which virtually outlaws mergers, the least costly takeover method. Other observable costs reflect superior management efficiency. Such costs either are not relevant to the issue of whether more federal regulation is needed or are a demonstration that shareholders are already well protected by market constraints. Caution is thus called for, since costs attributable to federal law or to management efficiency may well account for a significant portion of observable takeover costs. Other important costs may result from state

---

[48] Ibid., pp. 117–19.
[49] Manne and Wallich, *The Modern Corporation and Social Responsibility*, p. 17.
[50] See Manne, "Mergers and the Market for Corporate Control," p. 115.

24

legislation discouraging tender offers that appear to impair the efficiency of the market for management control. Whether federal regulation is necessary to reduce those costs raises issues quite different from those raised by the calls for federal intervention made by Cary and others. The question is dealt with in the next section.[51]

So far as the transaction costs of takeovers are concerned, protection for shareholders exists in the capital market, since corporations must offer a competitive return to attract capital. All investments involve transaction costs, such as the acquisition of information, and the competition between investment opportunities will direct investors to those transactions which have the least costs relative to the expected gain. The mere existence of transaction costs is not enough, therefore, to justify legal intervention.

Moreover, management is not a monolith but a group of persons who individually have little incentive to see their colleagues neglect their work or otherwise impair the corporation's efforts to be profitable.[52] The quest for advancement in a hierarchical structure necessarily creates a competitive atmosphere. Moreover, shirking duties and self-dealing reduce an individual's value in the job market because other firms look for different demonstrated qualities when hiring executives.

Still, takeovers do have high transaction costs. One might argue that management discretion which exists because of these costs is "unjustified"—another way of saying it can be eliminated without impairing firm efficiency. The difficulty is in distinguishing between the "unjustified" and the economically valuable since management discretion is closely related to stock price and thus to benefits (or the lack thereof) received by shareholders. Management can affect the share of corporate income which will be awarded to itself (whether salary, bonuses, lavish corporate accommodations, or lucrative sales or purchases with the corporations)—a fact that understandably disturbs many people. But the relevant discretion (excluding that subsidized by federal and, for the moment, state law) is also directly related, although not equal, to management's efficiency in maximizing profit on behalf of the firm. The management that generates the highest stock prices will also have the most discretion in the use of corporate assets. Whether that discretion results in rewards to management or gifts to charity, shareholders in the firm will also benefit

---

[51] See notes 98–100 below and accompanying text.
[52] See Armen A. Alchian, "Corporate Management and Property Rights," in *Economic Policy and the Regulation of Corporate Securities*, p. 337.

from the high stock price. Management discretion and shareholder benefit therefore move in the same direction.

Corporate critics balk at this analysis for a couple of reasons. One is that some simply don't like success in the marketplace.[53] A more responsible line of argument is that, although management discretion and shareholder benefit move together, some discretion could still be eliminated without necessarily impairing the efficiency of firms and reducing the benefits to shareholders.

Recent work on the theory of the firm by Armen Alchian and Harold Demsetz strongly suggests that the wholesale elimination of management discretion, rather than the definition and correction of particularized shareholder vulnerabilities, would be detrimental to shareholder interests.[54] Although the relation between marginal productivity and distribution of income is spelled out in economic theory, that theory simply assumes that economic organizations allocate rewards to resources according to their productivity. In short, the theory explains how various rewards are allocated to various firms according to output, but it does not explain how a similar allocative function is performed within the firm.

Alchian and Demsetz discuss how economic organizations (firms) meter input productivity and rewards so that rewards and output correspond. The problem is best illustrated by their example of two men who jointly lift heavy boxes into trucks.[55] The marginal productivity of each individual is very difficult to determine, and their joint product is not the sum of separable outputs. Obtaining information on individual marginal productivity and rewarding accordingly is at best very costly. In the absence of such information, however, there is an incentive to shirk because the reward to the individual is likely to be relatively unrelated to conscientiousness.

Moving from the example of the two men to the more complex case of the team effort of a firm, Alchian and Demsetz argue that an essential economic function of the firm is to monitor the various inputs in the team effort; in this way management meters marginal productivities and then takes steps to reduce shirking. Such monitoring

---

[53] Nader and his colleagues view "superior production techniques [and] managerial talent," which permit "established firms to maintain an absolute cost advantage," as a barrier to entry with which the antitrust laws ought to be concerned. No matter how long one ponders the point, it remains an anticompetitive and anticonsumer argument in that it penalizes the most efficient producers while protecting the least efficient. (Nader, p. 341.)

[54] Armen A. Alchian and Harold Demsetz, "Production, Information Costs, and Economic Organization," 62 *Amer. Econ. Rev.* 777 (1972).

[55] Ibid., p. 779.

requires that some group or individual within the firm be given the power to observe the performance of various input factors, to be the central party to all contracts with inputs, and to alter or discontinue their use. The monitor thus accumulates information on productivity through examination and experimentation, acts on that information, and polices inputs to reduce shirking.[56]

Because the monitor is a team member, a mechanism to meter *its* productivity and to reduce *its* incentive to shirk must also be created. Such a mechanism is to allocate to the monitor a share of the residual income left after other inputs have been paid. This arrangement encourages the monitor to promote the most efficient use of other inputs and to reduce shirking since its reward will vary according to its success in performing these tasks.[57]

Within the corporate framework, management—roughly speaking, the officers and "inside" directors—performs the monitoring function. Because of their obsession with the formal corporate legal structure in which the shareholders are "owners" and with the idea that the residual income share is associated with ownership, many commentators have concluded that management's discretion over corporate assets results in excessive compensation to management unrelated to its performance. If, however, management performs the monitoring function—if, in effect, it "owns" management control—the receipt of a residual share created by efficient performance is quite essential. The corporation's accumulation of capital from diffuse sources renders it impossible for investors to perform the monitoring function; it must be carried out by a centralized authority whose own reward and security in office are directly related to its productivity in metering inputs and reducing shirking. There is, therefore, sound reason for believing that a high return to shareholders and some management discretion over its own share are closely related.

In this regard management acts much like individual entrepreneurs, who also determine their share after making judgments about the hiring of inputs and the assets necessary to the long-run health of the firm. Unlike the individual proprietorship, however, corporations face the danger that management may care less about the long run than about quick enrichment at the price of permanently impairing the corporation. The threat of a subsequent takeover will not deter someone who is seeking such a one-shot gain. The economic constraints on corporate management thus leave shareholders vulner-

---

[56] Ibid., pp. 781–83.
[57] Ibid., p. 782.

able to the looting of corporate assets, a problem which generally does not concern the individual proprietorship. The legal restrictions on corporate management must be carefully drawn to reduce this vulnerability of shareholders and yet avoid reducing the residual share which contributes to the efficient performance of the monitoring function.

The Role of Law and Shareholder Protection

We return now to the costs and benefits of legal intervention. Consideration of what are proper legal rules will be by way of a general approach and illustration.

General Propositions. The corporation is a device that raises substantial amounts of capital and efficiently mixes this capital with other inputs. These inputs are directed and monitored by a management which increases its own return and maintains its security in office by keeping share price high—that is, by maximizing profit on behalf of the corporation. These functions can now be seen as largely independent of all but a few basic rules; they do not correspond to the apparent legal structure of "ownership" in the hands of shareholders and "unaccountable" discretion in the hands of management. If anything, management "owns" control, subject to being divested by the owners of common stock.

Although a variety of markets constrain management and create incentives for it to benefit shareholders, the corporate relation also creates substantial opportunities for fraud, self-dealing, and one-shot raids on corporate assets. The job of law is to reduce these opportunities in a way that benefits shareholders.

A wholly accurate weighing of the costs and benefits of every legal intrusion is, of course, not possible; and in a spectrum of alternatives, several may be correct. Out-of-hand rejection of a corporation code because it is less restrictive of management than codes of other states, however, is wholly uncalled for. Minimal restriction on management's discretion may maximize the yield to shareholders. Then again, it may not. But this uncertainty reflects only our ignorance about the effect of law, not the inherent worthiness of restrictions on management.

The Delaware code is thus not open to the kind of attack Cary and others have leveled at it. Although it lacks many restrictive provisions of older laws, not all limits on management have been removed. Basic protection for shareholders is written into the code,[58] and a

---

[58] See Resource Document on Delaware Corporation Law, in *Corporate Rights*, pp. 180–97.

fiduciary duty is imposed on management.[59] Moreover, unlike that of many states, Delaware procedure was for years geared to *facilitating* suits by shareholders since the *situs* of shares of a Delaware corporation was deemed to be Delaware. Stockholder plaintiffs were thus afforded means to obtain *quasi-in-rem* jurisdiction over nonresident directors. When the U.S. Supreme Court held this procedure unconstitutional, the Delaware legislature immediately passed a "consent" statute facilitating the obtaining of jurisdiction over corporate fiduciaries.[60] This act was a dramatic illustration of the centrality of enforcement to Delaware corporate law. In addition, Delaware does not require the posting of security for expenses and has eliminated other obstacles to shareholder litigation.[61]

Neither Delaware's code nor the case law interpreting it is perfect —no code is. Cases are often wrongly decided and statutes poorly drafted. A good legal system is always in evolution, and expectations of unvarying correctness are unrealistic. But in the case of corporation codes there is a mechanism which, over time, reasonably guarantees to shareholders and management alike a proper legal system to govern their relation in the capital market. That process is the very one reviled by proponents of federal intervention: competition among the states for corporate charters.

A state that rigs its corporation code so as to reduce the yield to shareholders will spawn corporations which are less attractive as investment opportunities than comparable corporations chartered in other states or countries, as well as bonds, savings accounts, land, and so on. Investors must be attracted before they can be cheated and, except for those seeking a one-shot, take-the-money-and-run opportunity to raid a corporation, management has no reason to seek out such a code. Just as shareholder yield and management discretion rise together, so too they may descend in tandem. Low yields to shareholders mean low stock prices, which mean low costs of takeover; and, as explained above,[62] such low costs reduce the parameters of management discretion. The chartering decision, therefore, so far

---

[59] See Keenan v. Ezhleman, 23 Del. Ch. 234, 2 A.2d 904 (Sup. Ct. 1938); Guth v. Loft, Inc., 22 Del. Ch. 255, 5 A.2d 503 (Sup. Ct. 1939); Johnston v. Greene, 35 Del. Ch. 479, 121 A.2d 919 (Sup. Ct. 1956).

[60] Shaffer v. Heitner, 433 U.S. 186 (1977); Del. Code §3114.

[61] Resource Document on Delaware Corporation Law, in *Corporate Rights*, p. 196. There is a broad right of inspection by shareholders, *Del. Code Ann.*, tit. 8, §220 (4 West Supp. 1968), including lists of stockholders, General Time Corp. v. Talley Indus. 43 Del. Ch. 531, 240 A.2d 755 (Sup. Ct. 1968).

[62] See notes 30–34 above and accompanying text.

as it concerns the capital market, favors those states that offer the optimal yield to both shareholders and management.

It is in neither management's nor the shareholders' interest to see a corporation's ability to raise capital impaired. As William Baumol has noted, even a relatively small need for capital from stock issues can impose discipline on a firm.[63] Moreover, raising capital through equity and through debt are closely related because both investors and lenders must make similar judgments about the long-run earning potential of the firm, and management's power to drain off assets obviously affects their judgment. In short, the lower the stock price, the higher the interest rate.[64]

The availability of internal financing does not affect this since the true cost of using retained earnings as capital is the opportunity cost, the highest return available in alternative uses. If an investment of retained earnings in another venture would return 15 percent, the true cost of using it within the firm is also 15 percent. Thus, an efficient firm which can borrow at 12 percent and invest retained earnings will earn more than the inefficient firm which can borrow only at 18 percent and must use retained earnings.

Considerations of the capital market make it not in the interest of management to seek out a corporate legal system that fails to protect investors, and the competition among states for charters is generally a contest to determine which legal system provides an optimal return to both interests. Only through that competition between legal systems can we perceive which legal rules are most appropriate for the capital market. Once a single legal system governs that market, we can no longer compare investor reaction. Ironically, in view of the conventional wisdom, the greater danger is not that states will compete for charters but that they will not.

More Power to Shareholders? The idea that more operational control of corporate affairs—such as initiating proposals, cumulative voting, requiring votes on some issues—should be placed in the hands of shareholders seemingly will not die, no matter how often it is dispatched by rational discussion.[65]

Corporate efficiency calls for decisional and operational processes wholly inconsistent with periodic, much less constant, intrusion by shareholders. Such intrusion not only reduces efficiency but also carries with it other costs, such as legal fees and increased personnel

---

[63] Baumol, *The Stock Market and Economic Efficiency*, p. 69.

[64] Note 38 above.

[65] Note 17 above.

needs, which the shareholders themselves must ultimately bear. It is notorious that the vast majority of shareholders in large corporations do not want the power to interfere in corporate affairs, would not use it if they had it, and do not regard themselves as corporate overseers. Instead, they quite sensibly view themselves only as investors whose "control" is in the stock market.

The calls for more power for shareholders are invariably made on behalf of tiny groups whose members happen not to view themselves solely as investors and who, like many of their academic supporters, are not particularly interested in maximizing the monetary yield to shareholders. On the contrary, campaigns such as Operation GM[66]—whatever their merits from society's point of view—seem necessarily antagonistic to investment interests.

It has even been argued that shareholders are simply more optimistic investors and less averse to risk than are bondholders and therefore need not be accorded any vote, their principal protection being in laws against fraud and the like.[67] Within the capital market this view may well be correct. It is confirmed by the existence of warrants and convertible preferred stocks which greatly resemble nonvoting shares of equity.[68] The operation of the market for management control, however, depends upon voting shares that have the power to replace an inefficient management and offer the opportunity for capital gains.

The calls of reform seem not to be based firmly on any theory of economic function or constraint, with the possible exception of proposals for stockholder votes on "fundamental changes."[69] These plans do not, however, seem highly prized by their supposed beneficiaries. State law does not prohibit corporations from adopting these reforms, but the demand by shareholders for their inclusion in corporate charters seems either satisfied or nonexistent. In the case of closely held corporations, the potential shareholders themselves are surely the best judges of what is appropriate to their needs, and they have the power to write whatever kind of charter they want. In the case of widely held corporations, it can be assumed that if institutional investors believed in the worthiness of such measures to any

[66] See Schwartz, "Towards New Corporate Goals."

[67] Alchian and Demsetz, "Production, Information Costs, and Economic Organization," p. 789, n. 14. See also Bayless Manning, "Book Review," 67 *Yale L. J.* 1477 (1958).

[68] Alchian and Demsetz, "Production, Information Costs, and Economic Organization," p. 789, n. 14.

[69] Melvin Aron Eisenberg, "The Legal Roles of Shareholders and Management in Modern Corporate Decisionmaking," 57 *Calif. L. Rev.* 1 (1969).

significant degree, the corporations would respond accordingly. Most of the proposals, after all, have been tried; if they benefited shareholders generally, the investment community would make that fact known to the corporate world. The lack of any such reaction is strong evidence that the trend of state law away from shareholder power is in the shareholders' interest.

Conflict of Interest Problems. A single-minded focus on legal structure accompanied by an indifference to economic function has generated considerable unease among legal commentators over the present law governing transactions between directors and the corporations they serve. Because directors are said to be fiduciaries and, like trustees, owe loyalty to the shareholders, transactions of the corporation which may profit directors are said to be tainted by a conflict of interest. Nineteenth-century law made all contracts in which a director was interested voidable at the instance of the corporation or shareholders no matter whether it was objectively fair.[70] Today, the law is dramatically different. Generally, no such contract is voidable if, after disclosure, it is adopted by a majority of disinterested directors or ratified by the shareholders, unless a court finds it unfair to the corporation, a standard far below that imposed on fiduciaries such as trustees.[71] This dramatic movement in corporate law is regarded by many critics as wholly unjustified and as a source of considerable financial injury to shareholders.[72]

For all the criticism, however, the shareholder losses are not visible to the naked eye. The trend away from earlier legal rules (effective during a period these same critics label the era of the robber barons) to those which prevail now has apparently not been accompanied by a corresponding decline in yield to shareholders or by investors turning away from this alleged legalized robbery. These nonevents are significant because few would doubt that similar changes in trust law would seriously injure trust beneficiaries and would lead to a greatly reduced use of that legal device—if not its disappearance. The failure of trust law to move in the same direction,

---

[70] Harold Marsh, Jr., "Are Directors Trustees? Conflict of Interest and Corporate Morality," 22 *Bus. Law.* 35, 36 (1966).

[71] Ibid., p. 43; Donald E. Schwartz, "The Need for Federal Chartering of Corporations," in *Federal Chartering for Large Corporations*, W. S. Moore, ed., (Washington, D.C.: American Enterprise Institute, forthcoming). If the contract is adopted by a majority of disinterested directors or ratified by the shareholders, the burden of demonstrating unfairness is on the plaintiff. Otherwise the defendant has the burden.

[72] See, for example, Nader, pp. 170–81; Schwartz, "The Need for Federal Chartering of Corporations."

moreover, may indicate that different economic forces are at work in the corporate area. The real problem is in the supposed analogy to trustees rather than in the competition for corporate charters.

Trustees by and large manage property within predetermined limits. Normally they operate under a trust instrument that directs their conduct and circumscribes their discretion as to risk, liquidity, and other factors. Their economic function is thus wholly dissimilar to that performed by corporate management. Although trustees may face decisions as to portfolio mix, they are not charged with the entirely different task of hiring the most efficient mix of productive inputs or with monitoring the use of these inputs so as to avoid shirking. Trustees do not maximize profit in the context of the competitive market for products and services. They do not concern themselves with innovation in products, methods of production and distribution, raising capital, or selecting personnel. Nor are they engaged in a team production effort that requires monitoring and the assignment of a residual share. Most important, trustees need not fear that beneficiaries may sell their interest to entrepreneurs who will install new trustees to manage the trust corpus. In short, trustees and corporate management have different economic functions and operate under completely different economic constraints. The movement of corporate law away from the strict trust analogy is the result, not of Delaware's perversity, but of flaws in the analogy.

As discussed earlier,[73] management's participation in determining its share of the enterprise's earnings creates powerful incentives to maximize profits and to keep the price of the company's stock high, just as the right to profits creates incentives for individual proprietors to manage their companies well. Because corporate management's discretion in determining its own share of the corporate return is directly related to the market for management control and stock price, these incentives benefit shareholders.

A single owner of an unincorporated business or general partners in a partnership also determine their share with an eye to what is necessary to hire capital, labor, and raw materials and to maintain a healthy competitive stature. There is no calculation by which a fixed sum or percentage of the gross business is allocated to these owners as their entitlement. Those who "own" management control in the corporate context operate under functionally similar circumstances which are obscured by some commenators' obsession with the shareholders' "ownership." The principal difference is simply that the fear

---

[73] See notes 51–57 above and accompanying text.

of looting is of no consequence in the case of the individual proprietorship (except perhaps to creditors which explains the existence of a body of law about fraudulent conveyances) while it is a serious risk in the case of corporations.

Facts cited by corporate critics actually support the view that a residual share to management may benefit shareholders. Ralph Nader and his associates, for example, chose to demonstrate the "excessive" compensation received by corporate management in an appendix listing the corporate-related income of the executives of the fifty largest corporations.[74] One supposes the critics chose these individuals because they are among the highest paid. Yet, if in fact management share and corporate or shareholder success go together, one would expect a rough correlation between size and executive compensation, at least to the extent that there is a rough correlation between size and earnings, and perhaps because of the more complex executive responsibility in sizable companies. The point the critics are seeking to make would be better proven by demonstrating a correlation between *low* stock price, *low* earnings, and *high* executive compensation. Moreover, most of the individuals cited also hold large blocks of stock in their corporations,[75] a most peculiar investment if state corporation law allows them freedom to divert corporate income directly to themselves.

A standard of fairness, of course, provides restraint only in egregious cases, but closer judicial scrutiny may not be consistent with economic function. Fairness in this context is based on more than personal values since it involves objective comparisons with commercial arrangements of a known arm's-length nature and the economic health of the enterprise. This is consistent with the foregoing economic analysis. The market constraints and incentives described operate only upon a management that views its future well-being in terms of a continuing relation with the corporation (or with another corporation impressed by prior performance) and thus has an interest in maintaining stock price and avoiding a takeover. High management compensation provides the incentive to bring about this happy result. Shareholder vulnerability exists where a management undertakes a one-shot raid on the corporate assets and impairs the corporation.

The fairness rule seems an attempt to recognize both the incentives for management to increase stock price and the vulnerability of shareholders to raids. It permits distribution of a residual share to the monitor (management) of team input but prohibits transactions

---

[74] Nader, pp. 567–91.
[75] Ibid.

that seem unlikely commercial arrangements when tested by arm's-length standards. The fairness rule is thus geared to economic function, in the hope of optimizing efficiency, rather than to legal analogy or the creation of a tidy legal structure for law professors.

To be sure, the fairness rule may permit some self-dealing unrelated to management efficiency. Like most legal rules, it may be in a process of evolution and only a crude form of regulation. A lack of fine tuning, however, is as characteristic of alternative solutions that are more restrictive and that run the risk of reducing managerial efficiency and misallocating managerial talent.

Alteration of Shareholders' Rights, Conflicts among Shareholders, and "Squeeze-Outs." A more promising area for corporate critics to attack lies in cases in which a shareholder or group of shareholders seem somehow to lose rights within the corporation which they might reasonably have viewed as indefeasible. Defeated expectations are, in a sense, "unfair." The preferred shareholder who finds his dividend arrearages eliminated in a recapitalization,[76] the shareholder who discovers that a merger has transformed his holdings into what he thinks is an inadequate amount of cash,[77] and the minority shareholder who believes the corporation is being operated by a dominant shareholder in a way that lessens his potential return[78]—all feel they have been deprived of the benefits of the deal they thought they were making. And so it may be. For example, majority interests, anticipating an increase in the value of the corporation's shares, might want to increase their holdings by altering or eliminating the interests of the minority.

On the other hand, of course, such transactions may be founded on business considerations which enhance—or are essential to—the competitive health of the corporation. A recapitalization may be necessary and impossible to accomplish if preferred claims to arrearages are fully honored. A merger may well bring about substantial cost savings. The health of the corporation may depend upon the elimination of an obstructionist and incompetent shareholder. And hard policy choices may simply have to be made by management no matter how strongly a minority holder disagrees.

The problem again is the trade-off between the benefits of elimi-

[76] Compare Keller v. Wilson & Co., 21 Del. Ch. 391, 190 A. 115 (Sup. Ct. 1936) with Havender v. Federal United Corp., 24 Del. Ch. 318, 11 A.2d 331 (Sup. Ct. 1940).

[77] Santa Fe Industries v. Green, 430 U.S. 462 (1977); Matteson v. Ziebarth, 40 Wash. 2d 286, 242 P.2d 1025 (1952).

[78] Sinclair Oil Corp. v. Levien, Del. Sup. 280 A.2d at 717 (1971).

nating *all* defeated expectations and the cost of injuring shareholders generally. Courts have had great difficulty resolving this dilemma for two reasons. First, the adjudicative process hampers the application of a general fiduciary duty in such cases. Fact-finding, for example, may be an intractable problem since both parties can conduct themselves with a view to future litigation and in ways which obscure their true motives. Majority interests may make it appear that a recapitalization (or whatever) is essential to the survival of the business although they privately believe a pot of gold is just around the corner. A minority interest may conceal an intent to blackmail under a contrived veil of suffering and defeated expectations. Any case involves uncertainties as to credibility, and where the prospective conditions of the economy and of particular markets are involved, the problems of proof expand geometrically.

Legal rules that seek to minimize such problems by giving one side or another rebuttable or conclusive presumptions may invite the unreasonable behavior they seek to control. For example, minority protection may prevent necessary recapitalizations and cost-saving mergers or paralyze corporate affairs by aiding obstructionist shareholders. The result is two groups with defeated expectations. Rules giving leeway to the majority, on the other hand, generate complaints of unfairness to minority interests.

The courts' second difficulty has been that in many circumstances no "fair" result exists. Consider the Delaware *Getty Oil* decision.[79] It permitted a parent company to continue to take advantage of its full quota of imported crude oil after a government agency had ruled that its subsidiary was not entitled to a quota of its own since it was controlled by the parent. Not to have allocated the quota between the two, Cary says, is unfair and an "abdication of responsibility by the court."[80]

Putting all the loss on the subsidiary is of course unfair, but putting part of the loss on the parent is also unfair because the administrative decision has created a no-win situation. All solutions seem arbitrary, and a pro rata allocation has no monopoly on justice. The underlying relation is consensual—no one is forced to become a shareholder—but there is no way for a court to know how the parties might resolve the issue through bargaining. The court's choice, therefore, is between substituting its concept of a good bargain and accepting the corporate structure's political resolution. Although loss-sharing may seem a good result for a court to impose on the parties,

---

[79] Getty Oil v. Shelly Oil Co., Del. Sup. 267 A.2d 883 (1970).
[80] Cary, p. 681.

the corporate structure is basically consensual. Either result, therefore, has merit so far as shareholder protection is concerned, since the loss is unavoidable and must be borne by some shareholders.

Establishing a fiduciary duty in the corporate context is exceedingly difficult once one moves beyond blatant self-dealing. Groups of shareholders frequently have conflicting interests and expectations which, when accommodated within the corporate political context, inevitably leave some feeling they have been treated unfairly. Those who would substitute the judgment of a court for the corporate decision would have a more persuasive case if they offered discernible and specific standards.

In an analogous area, the federal courts have generally declined to elaborate a pervasive fiduciary duty to displace internal resolutions by labor unions of issues in which the interests of groups of employees conflict. This is particularly significant because relations are far less consensual here than in the corporate case. Employees are barred by federal law from individual bargaining once a majority votes to be represented by a union, and constitutional overtones are thus present.[81] So long as discrimination on the basis of race or anti-union activities is not proven, the federal courts have been most reluctant to second-guess union decisions. In *Britt v. Trailmobile Co.*,[82] a case very similar to *Getty Oil*, a union in a merged company was allowed to put the employees of the acquired firm at the bottom of the enlarged seniority list, thereby giving junior employees of the acquiring company a significant advantage at the expense of senior employees of the other. Again, any result would be unfair to some, but since seniority is not based on merit but is principally an arbitrary standard to reduce employer discretion in the workplace,[83] the lack of discernible criteria induced the court to refrain from intervention.

The plight of the minority shareholder appears more bleak, moreover, than it really is. The quality of corporate management, for example, is an important determinant of the risk shareholders take in these regards, and potential shareholders can protect themselves in many circumstances merely by acting on available information. Many cases of "unfairness" to minority shareholders are isolated and unanticipated occurrences, caused as much by economic conditions as by foreseeable weakness of character in management. Moreover,

---

[81] Steele v. Louisville & N.R.R., 323 U.S. 192 (1944).

[82] 179 F.2d 569 (6th Cir. 1950), *cert. denied,* 340 U.S. 820 (1950).

[83] See Michael S. Jacobs and Ralph K. Winter, Jr., "Antitrust Principles and Collective Bargaining by Athletes: Of Superstars in Peonage," 81 *Yale L.J.* 1, 19–20 (1971).

management can change and liquidity problems may hamper shareholder exit. But there are other protections.

First, legal rules based on prior case law can be taken into account. Those who enter into transactions which do not pan out economically are not entitled to the same sympathy as those who lose out because of an unanticipated court ruling. The holder of preferred stock who sees dividend arrearages eliminated as a result of a court decision which shocks even members of the corporate bar[84] is to be pitied more than one who buys preferred stock under circumstances in which that sort of loss is a distinct possibility under established case law. The former incurred a risk for which he may not have bargained; the latter undertook a risk similar to the gamble taken by common shareholders on the future success of an enterprise. Even if the state court decisions are wrong, the impact is only on those who invested beforehand and cannot avoid them, not on those who invest later.

Second, many squeeze-outs and the like occur in corporations without many public shareholders.[85] In such cases, the participants know each other and have ample opportunity to protect themselves by charter provisions or by side contracts. Attempting to protect parties to such transactions through uniform federal rules would almost surely also restrict them in arranging their affairs to their own satisfaction. Such an attempt assumes the government knows better. We ought to tread cautiously in overriding the commercial arrangements of consenting adults.

Third, there are remedies in state law. The most egregious cases will fall under a general fiduciary duty imposed on those in control.[86] Where no business reason for the transaction appears, for example, the courts will protect the minority interests.[87] Other cases may fall within state remedial provisions such as appraisal statutes.[88]

The point here is not that the area is without difficulties but that protection is available both in private contractual arrangements and under state law. Dispute arises over the adequacy of particular state remedies and the relative costs and benefits of further judicial intrusion. If my more general point is correct, the competition between states for charters will eventually provide adequate remedies.

Consider further what kind of federal law would be appropriate.

---

[84] See Hottenstein v. York Ice Mach. Corp., 136 F.2d 944 (3d Cir. 1943).

[85] Joseph W. Bishop, "Book Review," 1976 *Duke L. J.* 155, 157.

[86] See David J. Greene & Co. v. Dunhill Int., Inc., Del. Ch. 249 A.2d 427 (1968).

[87] Singer v. Magnavox Co., 379 A.2d 1121 (Del. 1977).

[88] For example, *Del. Code Ann.*, tit. 8 §262 (West 1953).

If directed to the core of the problem, it would affect only publicly held corporations facing internal distributional questions about which there is no settled state judical precedent or statutory provision or for which state statutes have been inadequate. A general federal fiduciary duty is not a responsive remedy. Such responsibilities are already imposed under state law, and a federal statute of a general nature would simply not do what needs to be done: establish discernible standards accommodating conflicting interests in a way that does not damage the corporation but protects shareholders. If anything, a federal statute of a general nature would increase unpredictability—a move in exactly the wrong direction.

A general federal statute would also be an irresponsible delegation of the problem to the federal judiciary. It would be little more than a legislative declaration that state law is inadequate for unstated reasons and a plea for the federal judiciary to provide unspecified remedies for undefined problems. It is no insult to the federal judiciary to suggest that, if Congress believes state law inadequate, the intuitive values of federal judges are not the appropriate remedy. Indeed, it was as much the lack of discernible standards as congressional intent that induced the Supreme Court to eschew reading a general fiduciary duty into Rule 10b-5 in the *Santa Fe Industries* decision.[89]

For these and other reasons, Marvin Chirelstein has suggested federal legislative remedies that provide particularized rules for recurrent factual situations. Parent-subsidiary mergers would be subject to a requirement that only common stock be used to pay off minority interests in the subsidiary according to pre-merger stock-price ratios. Preferred arrearage recapitalizations would be subject to a relatively specific test.[90]

The Chirelstein approach is infinitely superior to invocations of "fairness" without decisional criteria.[91] Still, it seems more promising as an approach for state law than as a proposal for federal legislation. For one thing, the approach is no answer to the claim that shareholders cannot anticipate events undesirable to them since it provides solutions only after a problem has ripened, been analyzed, and been addressed by state courts. One may well ask how necessary a solution is at that point since parties are free to adjust their affairs to these court decisions without great costs. Nor is there reason to believe gov-

---

[89] See chapter 2, note 2 above and accompanying text.

[90] Marvin A. Chirelstein, "Legislative Solutions for Fiduciary Problems," in *Federal Chartering for Large Corporations*, W. S. Moore, ed. (Washington, D.C.: American Enterprise Institute, forthcoming).

[91] See notes 19–23 above and accompanying text.

ernment is better than private parties in anticipating events affecting their consensual arrangements.

Another problem with Chirelstein's proposal is that he has more confidence in his approach than in his solutions. He concedes he is uncertain how to weigh business expediencies against minority expectations. He qualifies his call for the substitution of "good legal solutions for deficient ones" with the condition that we be able to "decide which is which."[92] But if the right solution is in doubt, the case for this particular kind of federal legislation collapses. If we do not know which solution is correct, then we risk substituting a deficient federal rule for a process of state experimentation which can be expected to move toward optimal solutions. State rules are also more easily changed than federal ones, and the competition between states for charters provides safeguards which are lost with federal legislation. The Chirelstein approach is therefore sound, but only if carried out at the state level.

Of Outside Directors. Concern over the power of corporate officers and "inside" directors has prompted a number of proposals for legal structures to check that power. Some have called for greater supervision of management by institutional investors which hold large blocks of stock.[93] Others—and more frequently today—call for a requirement that corporate boards have a majority of "outside" directors.[94]

It should be said straight out that outside directors—including those designated by large institutional shareholders—can perform important functions in the areas in which shareholders are most vulnerable. They are, for example, an element of protection against a take-the-money-and-run management. They are a check on self-dealing, fraud, and excessive compensation. They can insist on proper auditing procedures and review corporate decisions of a magnitude sufficient to entail the risk of foul play. Furthermore, outside directors have a perspective different from that of people who are immersed in the corporation's affairs. They can provide helpful analysis in decision making, asking tough questions about a proposal which even a fully conscientious management may not face directly because of an unconscious pride of authorship.

Beyond these important but limited functions, however, what

---

[92] Chirelstein, "Legislative Solutions for Fiduciary Problems."

[93] J. A. Livingston, *The American Stockholder* (Philadelphia: Lippincott, 1958).

[94] *Corporate Rights*, statement of Harvey J. Goldschmid, p. 246; also statement of Detlev F. Vagts, p. 339; statement of Robert H. Mundheim, p. 218; statement of Peter Peterson, p. 103; statement of A. A. Sommer, Jr., p. 56.

can realistically be expected of outside directors is a matter of some doubt.[95] Management's knowledge and experience in the corporation's affairs must always be superior to those who play a part-time role and receive part-time compensation. The resources available to management in terms of staff and other useful perquisites are also so superior to those available to outsiders that the latter must inevitably give great weight to management proposals.

Corporate critics really do not challenge this analysis so much as avoid it by calling for measures to strengthen the hand of outside directors.[96] Give them more pay, provide them with a staff, require them to spend more time on corporate business, and so on. But such measures do not provide an independent check on management discretion so much as they duplicate and relocate the very same discretion. An outside director, after all, will never be on an equal footing with management until he spends a comparable amount of time, receives comparable compensation, and has comparable resources at his disposal. Then, however, he is in every sense an inside director.

The issue evaded by the critics is the definition of functions to be performed by outside directors. One cannot catalogue the necessary resources until the job description is completed. This requires a differentiation, rather than duplication, of functions; and outside directors must be assigned functions other than a wholesale second-guessing of management, if for no other reason than the relative inferiority of their information and knowledge (so long as they do not become "insiders"). It would surely stand matters on their head to locate operating authority in the least knowledgeable directors.

The first question is thus "What should they do?" not "What do they do it with?" The remedies offered by the corporate critics assume that the function of outside directors is essentially the same as inside directors and seek only to provide them with comparable responsibilities and resources. This does not solve the problem of the unaccountability of management power; it merely relocates it so the corporate critics of 1998 will have a fresh target for their sport. Until our present band of corporate critics answers the first question and defines functions for outsiders going beyond those listed above, the remedies they cry for must necessarily be beside the point. If outside directors are to oversee auditing functions, for example, then the resources necessary to the independent performance of this func-

---

[95] See Myles L. Mace, "The President and the Board of Directors," *Harvard Business Review* (January-February, 1972), p. 37.

[96] *Corporate Rights*, statement of Harvey J. Goldschmid, p. 246; statement of Roderick Hills, pp. 304–5.

tion should be provided. But that tailors the resources to a discrete responsibility.

Federal regulation, moreover, seems inappropriate since a realistic appraisal of the function of outside directors must be made case by case. Corporations troubled by fraud may need a substantial majority of outsiders. Corporations in industries in which scarce technological or other elaborate and complex knowledge is important may be unable to afford a substantial number of outside directors. Variations abound among industries, markets, and firms (a point academics are usually insensitive to, until government does to universities what it has routinely been doing to business), and any attempt to impose a general rule through federal legislation is not likely to benefit shareholders generally. This does not, of course, preclude state corporation codes or private bodies such as stock exchanges from imposing such a requirement.[97]

Nor is economic inefficiency the only danger. I am personally persuaded that publicly held corporations should have outside audit committees. Were such a requirement imposed by federal law, however, there would be an overwhelming temptation to expand the responsibilities of such a committee, either in the process of administration or by amendment, far beyond its original justification, and to make it the tool of government or other extracorporate forces.

Takeover Statutes: Monopolization in the Market for Management Control. State statutes which severely impede takeovers impair the constraints imposed by the interrelations of the capital market, product market, and market for corporate control. Central to the efficient working of the latter is minimizing the transaction costs of corporate takeovers, including costs imposed by law. To the extent that state law increases these costs, it increases management's discretion and in a way that does not benefit shareholders.

The question then is whether takeover statutes are a proper issue for federal regulation. So far, I have argued that product-market competition, the competition for capital, and management's self-interest in seeking to increase its own share channel the chartering decision toward those legal arrangements that optimize the management-shareholder relation. When competition exists in the product and capital markets, management's self-interest alone leads it to seek such legal arrangements. Critical to this process is the competition among states for corporate charters and free competition in the market for management control.

---

[97] Ibid., statement of Roderick Hills, pp. 326–27.

There are critical differences between legal issues that involve shareholder power, conflicts of interest, and fiduciary problems, and those raised by takeover statutes. The former issues pertain to the regulation of the capital market, which, given the range of alternatives available to potential investors, management cannot even partially monopolize without *federal* regulation. Takeover statutes, however, although they involve trading in shares, regulate the market for management control and may well serve as a vehicle for monopolization even at the state level. To be sure, like a state law permitting embezzlement, a takeover statute will affect share price and the ability of relevant corporations to raise capital. Product-market competition will then exert pressure on shareholders and management to seek other legal arrangements. In existing corporations, however, management cares about success in product competition and in keeping stock price high only because it is management; takeovers directly threaten that role. Losing one's position as management will seem much less desirable than whatever injury may occur to the corporation as a result of a state takeover statute. In these circumstances, profit maximizing on behalf of the corporation—that is, providing for easy takeovers— may not be in management's economic self-interest.

The competition among states for charters may provide inadequate protection in the case of takeover statutes. Existing management of many corporations can be expected to lobby for such laws, and the ability to reincorporate without difficulty may pressure states into passing takeover statutes to prevent or to induce reincorporation. The fact that such statutes are usually applicable only to larger companies suggests that much of the pressure is from existing rather than proposed firms.[98] One ought not overstate the case, however, since competition in the product and capital markets exerts pressure in the other direction. Some managements may well feel secure without such legal protection, and they may prosper. New ventures needing to attract capital, moreover, will not feel as free to seek out such laws as the management of existing corporations. This may explain why Delaware's takeover statute is one of the least burdensome. It provides only for a twenty-day notice period and a twenty-day offer period without a hearing, and it allows opting out by charter provision (of particular relevance for new corporations).

The extent to which the competition for charters protects shareholders in the case of takeover statutes is inconclusive. This is not a serious analytic problem, however, since takeover statutes are only peripherally a chartering issue. Takeover laws apply not only to cor-

---

[98] Wilner and Landy, "The Tender Trap," p. 8.

porations chartered in a state but to all firms that have their principal offices there. Because they apply even when all shareholders reside elsewhere or are scattered among the states, the competition for charters is not the significant factor in the state's legislative judgment. For example, a widget manufacturer in State A may lobby A's legislature for takeover legislation even though the firm is chartered in State B and the public shareholders are scattered. Politically, legislators in A may believe they have little to lose by protecting local management, while the absence of takeover provisions in B does not significantly increase revenues from chartering because B's corporation code appears to be overridden by A's takeover legislation. Takeover statutes therefore appear to be analogous to laws protecting local businessmen, such as taxicab owners, from competition. Since competition for management control is in fact interstate, takeover laws may violate the Commerce Clause.[99]

The extraterritorial features of takeover statutes restrain the competition among state legal systems for corporate charters. The fact that such measures are employed strongly suggests that the capital market does exert pressures which encourage states to provide optimal legal systems. Were the conventional wisdom correct— or even the limited view expressed here as to the relation between that competition and takeover legislation—extraterritoriality would be unnecessary.

There is, therefore, a case for federal regulation protecting competition in the market for management control. In fact, regulation of tender offers (perhaps the wrong kind) exists in the Williams Act,[100] which, in addition to constitutional issues arising out of the Commerce Clause, may preempt the state laws.

The Role of Federal Law in Shareholder Protection

This chapter has argued two propositions: (1) The competition among states for charters will tend toward optimal legal systems regulating the market for capital. (2) Existing state corporation law (except for takeover statutes which are extraterritorial and monopolize a different market) is, in light of economic theory, consistent with what seems an optimal solution. If either proposition is correct, the likelihood of the other also being correct is very high. If either proposition is correct, moreover, the calls for federal intervention are wrong.

An expanded federal role in corporate governance would almost

---

[99] See ibid., pp. 8, 15.
[100] Note 45 above and accompanying text.

surely be counterproductive. At the federal level, there is no mechanism by which optimal legal rules governing the shareholder-corporation relation can be determined. One must thus turn to the proposals put forth by the advocates of further intervention. These suggestions are at best academic guesswork in which investors themselves are palpably disinterested; at their worst, they are generalized calls for more regulation which fail to spell out details.

There is more than a little evidence that to advocates of federal regulation shareholder protection is a catch phrase behind which parade a variety of measures designed principally to increase the role of the public sector at the expense of the private. The most striking thing about this movement is that it exists, if at all, only in extremely isolated pockets in the investment community. Its principal support is among academics and self-designated consumer advocates whose attachment to the private sector is suspect and whose concern for corporate success is downright negative. How else explain why proposals for more rigorous control of management in the name of shareholder protection are routinely coupled with proposals which are wholly antithetical to the interests of shareholders? Thus, after excoriating Delaware for injuring shareholders, Cary suggests, "We might go even farther and ask what representation the modern constituency of the corporation—employees, consumers and the public, as well as shareholders—should have in the governance of the corporation."[101] Such proposals do not represent going "farther" so much as a radical change in direction. And Nader, whose relationship to the investment community has resembled a holy war, joins his "shareholder protection" proposals to the usual potpourri of antibusiness measures.[102] Such "reformers" can be expected to protect investors much as foxes liberate chickens.

The track record of the federal government does not evidence much sympathy even for measures which would clearly benefit shareholder interests. The strongest case for federal intervention would be in the realm of increasing competition or reducing transaction costs in the market for management control. Federal merger policy, and probably the Williams Act as well, strongly suggest, however, that sympathy for competition in that market is not very strong at the federal level.

Once federal legislation is enacted, it will be very difficult to correct, no matter how wrong it may be. Not only will bureaucrats view the legislation as a cornerstone of the Republic and perhaps

---

[101] Cary, p. 701.
[102] Compare Nader, pp. 86–227, with pp. 228–389.

seek to expand its jurisdiction and their own, but even the most demonstrably foolish rule will lead to calls for more rather than less regulation. Because federal legislation is not in direct competition with other legal systems, the behavior of investors under differing rules cannot be observed, and we can only theorize about which rules optimize the underlying economic relation. Federal intervention in the name of shareholder protection should be undertaken only after a need for it has been demonstrated and the proposal at hand has been clearly shown to meet that need. At present, the case for federal intervention (except for takeover statutes) lacks both a thoretical and empirical basis. Worse, it finds its sole political sustenance in a movement that has little sympathy for shareholders as investors or for the survival of the private sector in general.

3

The Social Control
of Corporate Power

The Concerns of the Critics and Their Proposals

For the very reasons that federal regulation of corporate governance is an inappropriate means of optimizing relations between investors and corporate management, state legislation is an inappropriate device to influence corporate governance in the name of social interests. It has been argued here that competitive legal systems allow parties to corporate capital transactions to choose the most efficient legal structure for their purposes. Because social control expressly requires that private interests be overridden—that a legal structure which is avowedly inefficient from the parties' point of view be imposed—competitive state legal systems inevitably work against the goal of social control.

The question then is not whether the controls should be federal or state but what changes in corporate governance are appropriate on their merits. Although the demands for congressional scrutiny are frequently marked by urgency and even stridency,[1] the concerns of the critics about corporate performance appear not to be limited to well defined antisocial conduct which seems uniquely regulable by changes in the mechanisms of corporate governance. Rather, they bespeak a more general and rather undifferentiated concern with the power of corporations.

Thus, A. A. Sommer, Jr., while a commissioner of the SEC, keynoted a symposium on corporate law with the following statement of what he conceives to be the problem:

---

[1] See, for example, notes 4–5 below and accompanying text.

The people who control [corporations] . . . have the power to decide whether a plant will be closed, thus impoverishing a community; to decide to curtail production, thereby adding massively, in some instances, to the rolls of the unemployed, thus creating a problem for the political bodies; to blunder and thereby harm the interests of those depending upon the prosperity of the enterprise for jobs, dividends, security. Running through all this is an abiding misgiving in the American mind about any power, whatever its form or source.[2]

In a similar vein, Donald Schwartz of the Georgetown Law School, a frequent advocate of extensive federal regulation, has written:

Criticism from the reformers is directed to the great concentration of economic power in the hands of relatively few corporations. That concentration of power is of itself something to fear; but, in addition, it is claimed that corporate conduct has worked against the public interest in such areas as pollution, minority opportunity, the war, product safety, and generally, in fulfilling society's needs.[3]

Not to be outdone, Nader and some associates have declared:

So today, while the United States Constitution governs every federal, state, county and local authority, no matter how small, it is silent about the giant corporations which govern our economy. . . .
   Mere brobdingnagian size, however, only begins an analysis of corporate power. Herbivorous dinosaurs were also huge—but weak, dumb and helpless before predators. Our giant firms, on the other hand, have both size *and* power. A couple of hundred corporate managers, who could fit comfortably into a small auditorium, can make decisions controlling most of our industrial economy.[4]

According to Nader and his associates, the Brobdingnagians levy "invisible taxes" in the way of pollution, the introduction of toxic substances, discrimination, "white-collar blues," overweening political power, the invasion of privacy, "local sway," deceptive information, unsafe products, the danger of undue reliance on technology, economic concentration, the undesirable conduct of multinational "worldcorps," the concentration of wealth and income, and business crime,

---

[2] A. A. Sommer, Jr., "A Keynote Address—of Sorts," 31 *Bus. Law* 871–72 (1976).
[3] Donald E. Schwartz, "Federal Chartering of Corporations: An Introduction," 61 *Geo. L. Rev.* 71, 72–73 (1972).
[4] Nader, pp. 2–3.

all of which (not including acne), they conclude, can be avoided by the federal chartering of corporations.[5]

The concern over corporate power purports to be a concern over centralized power analogous to the theme of the Federalist Papers.[6] The content of the criticism is by no means restricted to the economic impact of the corporation.[7] Rather it concerns itself with the "comprehensive economic-social-political power"[8] of large corporations, and particularly the discretion of corporate management in wielding such power.

Some proposals might work significant change in corporate behavior and deserve to be considered. These fall into three categories. The first would create legal mechanisms by which groups affected by corporate decisions—workers, consumers, suppliers, residents of neighboring towns or cities, and the public generally—would be represented somehow in decision making.[9] The second would require corporations to make public disclosure of such matters as hiring policy (for example, the number of blacks, women, or other minorities), occupational health data (such as toxic substances in the work place), cost data, information on activities causing pollution, market-share data, line of business data and more.[10] The third would regulate the mechanisms of corporate governance with a view to improving existing economic regulation.[11]

Representation of Groups Affected by Corporate Decisions

There are basically two nonmarket devices by which "affected" groups (somehow defined) may be directly represented in the corporate decision making process. First, representatives of a group may be put on

---

[5] Ibid., pp. 5–25, 86–414.

[6] Abram Chayes, "The Modern Corporation and the Rule of Law," in *The Corporation in Modern Society*, Edward S. Mason, ed. (Cambridge, Mass.: Harvard University Press, 1959), pp. 25, 38–39; Morton Mintz and Jerry S. Cohen, *America, Inc.* (New York: Dell, 1971), pp. 15–16; Sommer, "A Keynote Address," p. 872; see also Nader.

[7] See Richard J. Barber, *The American Corporation* (New York: E. P. Dutton, 1970); Mintz and Cohen, *America, Inc.*; Harry M. Trebing, ed., *The Corporation in the American Economy* (New York: Franklin Watts, 1970).

[8] Schwartz, "Federal Chartering of Corporations," p. 78.

[9] See, for example, Chayes, "The Modern Corporation and the Rule of Law"; Nader, pp. 207–10.

[10] See, for example, *Corporate Rights*, statement of Dr. Gordon Adams, p. 25ff; Nader, pp. 215–99.

[11] See, for example, Nader, pp. 300–89; Christopher D. Stone, *Where the Law Ends* (New York: Harper & Row, 1975).

the board of directors. Second, certain corporate decisions may be subject to special procedures, up to and including a vote by "affected" groups outside the corporation.

The first group of proposals, which may be labeled constituent representation plans, would place representatives of labor, ultimate consumers, commercial consumers, suppliers, and the "public" on boards of directors.[12] Were these representatives placed on boards in sufficient numbers and imbued with sufficient aggressiveness—which is not inevitable, it should be said—corporate behavior would be greatly affected and the law of the internal governance of the corporation revolutionized.

It is hard to understand why many people who decry shareholder weakness as a result of the "separation of ownership and control" seize upon these proposals as appropriate for serious consideration.[13] One thing that is clear is that the principal effect of these proposals would be to increase profoundly the separation of shareholders and management. If constituent directors are to represent nonshareholder groups in corporate decisions, then any fiduciary duty of theirs must be to those constituencies and not to shareholders. If a "labor" director is to care only about maximizing profit on behalf of the corporation, it seems hardly worth the effort to change the existing system. It is thus implicit in the proposals for constituent representation that the "separation of ownership and control" will become a complete break.

The elimination of a fiduciary duty to shareholders, moreover, must apply to the whole board rather than to just the constituent directors. If some directors are placed on boards by legal fiat and are legally free, if not affirmatively bound, to make proposals antagonistic to shareholder interests, other directors must be legally free to accept them. This in turn means that the discretion of corporate management, the original raison d'être for constituent representative proposals, is likely to increase rather than diminish. To the extent that constituent representatives control a board, they will protect an accommodating management from takeovers, and the market mechanisms described earlier will not function. Rewards to management in such circumstances will depend more on its retaining the favor of nonshareholder

---

[12] Chayes, "The Modern Corporation and the Rule of Law"; see also Cary, p. 701. Compare Phillip I. Blumberg, "Reflections on Proposals for Corporate Reform Through Change in the Composition of the Board of Directors: 'Special Interest' or 'Public' Directors," 53 *Boston U. L. Rev.* 547 (1973); David L. Ratner, "The Government of Business Corporations: Critical Reflections on the Rule of 'One Share, One Vote,' " 56 *Corn. L. Rev.* 1 (1970).

[13] See, for example, Cary.

groups than on maximizing profit on behalf of the corporation. Management might bargain with these other groups for quid pro quos which exceed the reward available in the orthodox corporate situation. For example, it has been reported that labor representatives on the boards of German corporations have formed alliances with management against large shareholders and shareholder representatives.[14]

Corporate critics do not really address the fiduciary duty issue or the difficulty of fashioning legal rules to govern the behavior of directors on a board which includes groups whose interests are openly antagonistic to those of the shareholders. German law has wrestled with this problem in a way which has exposed the inconsistency between loyalty to the corporation and representation of constituent groups, but it has been unable to reach a coherent resolution of the issue.[15] With such a fundamental question left up in the air, it would be rash for American law to move in the direction of constituent directors.

The literature also ignores other threshold problems raised by constituent representation. If suppliers and commercial purchasers are in fact represented on the board—with auto companies represented on steel company boards and vice versa, for example—there must be some communication between them and their representative director. This representative director must then take a position as to trading terms for dealing with the corporation. There is a phrase for this kind of conduct in another branch of the law: price fixing, a per se violation of section 1 of the Sherman Act.[16] The representation of all buyers and sellers on boards would be a centralizing, anticompetitive force; if effective, it would result in a pervasive system of bilateral monopoly. Monopolization and the further centralization of power would result. The model for this form of corporate decision making is neither democratic government nor the Federalist Papers but Italian fascism and the National Recovery Administration. Rarely, indeed, have proposals from serious people had so little relation to the ends they are said to further and so much recent history to refute them.

As for so-called public members, the literature calling for their appointment fails to specify the criteria by which their actions are to be guided. If added to corporate boards in sufficient numbers, they could become a lawless force which might simply rubber-stamp management, be wholly obstructionist, or represent the interests of

---

[14] Detlev Vagts, "Reforming the Modern Corporation: Perspectives from the German," 80 *Harv. L. Rev.* 23, 73 (1966).

[15] Ibid., pp. 74–75.

[16] Compare United States v. Soconoy-Vacuum Oil Co., 310 U.S. 150 (1940).

whatever groups are politically powerful at the time, all of which would be within their discretion. The critics never face this issue, probably since facing it would compel them to define the "public interest," or at least the processes by which it is to be discovered. These tasks might reveal that beneath all that righteous indignation is neither political nor economic theory, only boundless antagonism to the private sector.

Nor do the corporate critics spell out how to define relevant constituencies. Are only existing suppliers, customers, and workers to be represented, or are all potential members of such groups also to be heard? If only existing suppliers, customers, and workers are represented, we can anticipate that the entry of competitors and newcomers will be restricted because corporate boards control corporate contracts. Again, the proper analogy is not to the Federalist Papers but to the stifling of competition under the National Recovery Administration.

One of the attractive features of free markets is that potential entrants need not be administratively identified in advance; they appear automatically as profitable opportunities present themselves. Although unidentified, they are nevertheless "affected" by corporate decisions which might tempt them to offer to become a supplier or whatever, and the failure to represent potential suppliers and similar groups on boards would vitiate much of the purpose of constituent representatives. There are no reliable administrative means by which these unidentified groups can be accurately identified, however. Were an "affected" group to be identified, processes to choose its representative would have to be established. The spacious room for bizarre proposals this task opens up is infinite. Shall we have a rule of one person, one vote, or shall we attempt to take the magnitude of interest into account? Who picks the "consumer" representative? In truth, no methods are available to choose genuine representatives. The failure of corporate critics even to address the issue demonstrates how casual—not to say thoughtless—their proposals are.

The economic naiveté of this genre of proposals is demonstrated by the call for procedures allowing affected groups to vote on corporate conduct. Towns affected by pollution, for example, would be allowed to vote on whether the polluter must cease,[17] and towns from which a company desires to move its plant would be permitted to vote on whether it may go. Totally ignored are the economic interrelations that extend the "affected" groups far beyond the political unit specified. A swank suburb ought not be able to close down an urban

---

[17] See Nader, pp. 207–10.

plant, employing several hundred poor people and producing a product valued by hundreds of thousands of consumers. And one town should not be able to inhibit another from industrializing by preventing a company from moving, no matter how uneconomic it may be to remain. In the case of pollution, regulation that makes a cost-benefit judgment and takes all interests into account is necessary. In the case of plant removal, a competitive economy surely depends on the removal, rather than the imposition of, artificial barriers to the mobility of economic resources. The effects on consumers of the critics' proposals would be those of a tariff, and those who call for their adoption must abandon even the pretense of concern for consumers.

If government were to adopt any such radical proposals, it would inevitably be sucked in to prevent inevitable bankruptcies and to provide the capital which private sources would no longer invest. The Lockheed loan, said to be justified because of the company's position as a defense contractor, will serve not as an example of a mistake but as a precedent for an expanded agenda of government support for business.

Corporations forced to operate under such schemes will not be able to attract capital, debt, or equity, and to the extent that their physical assets are of value only to similarly governed organizations their market value would fall precipitously. The result would be an increase in prices to consumers, rising unemployment, and a general decline in the standard of living. At a time when capital formation is a fundamental problem threatening the entire economy, the very making of such proposals seems irresponsible.

The idea of constituent directors has not been thought out, and, even its most obvious implications have not been seriously addressed by its advocates. That it continues to be bandied about strongly suggests that many of the corporate critics either are interested in punitive rather than remedial measures—or, more charitably, are profoundly ignorant of the economy.

Disclosure of Corporate Affairs

Part of the call for widespread change in modes of corporate governance looks to increased disclosure of information about corporations.[18] The material sought is exceedingly diverse and voluminous.

One area of disclosure would be the corporate financial struc-

---

[18] See note 10 above; see also Stone, *Where the Law Ends*, pp. 199–216.

ture.[19] Actual stock ownership would be made public, as would information about subsidiaries and joint ventures. Other commercial affiliations of owners and directors would also be disclosed. Corporations would be made to reveal outstanding debts and other contractual arrangements, including information about the parties to them. Uniform accounting procedures, including "line-of-product" reporting, would be mandatory.

Social impact data would also be required.[20] Environmental information concerning air and water emissions, attempts to control pollution, the nature of manufacturing processes, energy consumption, and litigation involving such matters would be collected and published. So would current antidiscrimination efforts or litigation and employment statistics for each job description by race, sex, and salary. Occupational safety and health information, data about corporate political activities, extensive materials on the acquisition and performance of military contracts (such as information on employment of retired members of the armed services, former employees in the government, size of military business, subcontracting), cost data, and overseas sales would all be available to the public.

The benefits to be derived from the Everest of paper these proposals would generate are said to be investor protection, increased social accountability, efficient law enforcement, and improved legislative processes. No doubt there would be benefits in each of these areas, but evaluating the net effect requires attention to costs as well as to benefits.

The costs of such a program would be high indeed. Only a fraction of the required information is presently maintained by firms in useable form. The rest would have to be collected in gross from every plant, department, division, or whatever of each firm; relevant material would then be distilled, put in an appropriate order and form, checked, reproduced, and distributed. At every step, from the bottom of the company to the top, complicated legal advice would be necessary to establish the adequacy of each filing.

While the costs of these proposals are extravagant and certain, their benefits seem erratic. It makes no sense to exempt any significant corporation—marginal businesses, after all, may be under more insistent financial pressure to pollute, endanger workers or even bribe officials than the fabled Brobdingnagians. But only a fraction of the

---

[19] *Corporate Rights*, statement of Dr. Gordon Adams, pp. 27–28; Nader, pp. 286–96.

[20] *Corporate Rights*, statement of Dr. Gordon Adams, p. 28; Nader, pp. 228–59.

mountain of paper produced will ever be read. No doubt some congressional committee will gain some insight into some areas of corporate behavior, some law enforcement officials will spot evidence of an illegal act, and anticorporate publicists will find some good copy. If the experience of the Food and Drug Administration is any guide, however, the principal readers of these reports will be business competitors. So far as the general public is concerned, the increase in information it receives will depend largely on who reads the materials and what is distilled for mass readership.

Even so, much relevant information is not called for by the present proposals. If social impact is to be taken seriously, for example, information should be published to indicate how much higher retail prices are as a result of government regulation (including the required disclosure) and how many jobs are lost through taxation. Such matters are quite as relevant as the material corporate critics call for.

The benefits to be gained from wholesale disclosure thus seem sporadic and incomplete. In return, however, every consumer who purchases a product from a corporation subject to such provisions would have to pay higher prices, thus decreasing sales and reducing employment. Great amounts of resources such as labor and timber would be diverted from consumer wants (and pollution generated) in order to fuel the vast production of unread paper.

It seems likely, too, that a relatively heavy burden would fall on small business if these proposals were adopted. There are large start-up costs associated with wholesale disclosure—new staff, legal advice, and the reorganization of record keeping, for instance—and economies of scale as well. If the cost of legal advice does not vary proportionately with the volume of data recorded, the marginal cost to small business of wholesale disclosure may be substantially greater than to bigger firms. This result is generally inconsistent with other proposals of corporate critics. For government to impose costs which larger firms can meet relatively more cheaply than smaller ones is an odd proposal for those who generally preach against economic concentration.

The point here is not that disclosure has no net benefits. Of course it may, but they depend very much on what is to be disclosed, how much it will cost, and why it is needed. Disclosure can be justified case by case, not on the undifferentiated wholesale grounds suggested by the critics. Where an articulated governmental policy exists, or where a new policy is being considered, the appropriate congressional committee, regulatory agency, or law enforcement body usually has, or ought to have, the power to seek information necessary to the performance of its functions. This rifle-shot approach, which ensures that the particular information is desired by someone who is likely to read it, is better than a wholesale approach which produces a largely unread, useless deluge of paper at the price of a severe tax on consumers.

Law Enforcement and Corporate Governance

Some proponents of federal chartering for corporations attempt to connect regulatory issues with issues of corporate governance.[21] They have claimed that pollution control, elimination of employment discrimination, antitrust enforcement, bribery control, and the like can be enhanced by the federal chartering of corporations.

This claim is odd because an ample assortment of legal remedies, both traditional and novel, are available in the absence of chartering. Fines, injunctions, trustees, monitors, prison sentences, and other remedies may be invoked to regulate the conduct of state-chartered corporations. Much of the discussion of remedies against corporate misconduct suggests that these traditional methods are inadequate. For example, it has been argued that a $7 million civil penalty for pollution will not affect the behavior of a company the size of Ford Motor Company.[22] If $7 million is less than the revenue generated by the pollution, it may well be that Ford will continue to pollute. But that merely indicates that the penalty should be larger. If the argument is that a $7 million penalty does not matter to a large company, that is not plausible. Even if it is assumed that a several million dollar loss would not affect the firm's position in the capital market and the market for management control, why would management allow such a sum to go to the government when it could with impunity enrich itself?[23] Traditional remedies seem, therefore, ample.

Chartering offers the additional remedial device of revocation of the charter and the right to do business. But that is so Draconian, not only for corporate management but for workers, suppliers, and customers as well, that it is doubtful that it would ever be used. If so, chartering adds nothing to the traditional regulatory measures and is somewhat irrelevant to social control.

Christopher Stone has argued that in certain carefully defined situations direct intrusion on corporate governance may greatly facil-

---

[21] Chapter 1, note 2.

[22] Stone, *Where the Law Ends*, pp. 47–48.

[23] See chapter 2, note 29 and accompanying text.

itate social control.[24] Any large bureaucratic structure has bottlenecks which make it unresponsive in certain ways. Where legal penalties do not seem severe, the kind of pressure needed to generate a response may not be forthcoming from a top management occupied by a variety of other responsibilities or from lower-level officials who do not feel under great pressure.

In general Stone rejects proposals for public directors, but he argues for the judicial appointment of such directors in two situations: (1) where repeated delinquency by a corporation has been demonstrated, and (2) where a serious generic problem exists in the industry. In the first situation, when repeated violations of the law demonstrate a persistent defect in the mechanisms of corporate control, a court-appointed director would serve as an in-house probation officer. He would have the power to go back to the court for an order directed to specific individuals within the corporation to take the necessary steps. In the second situation, no violations of the law need be shown, only a "problem" peculiar to the industry: for instance, high susceptibility of employees to cancer, or high pollution. The court-appointed directors would be empowered to investigate the problems, work out alternative corrective measures to present to the board, and serve as a liaison with government. A change in policy need not result if the costs of avoidance seem prohibitive, but the board will at least be apprised of the social costs of the business.

The Stone approach is attractive because the public directors have responsibilities tailored to specific corporate problems and a specific limited time in which to work them out, rather than a diffuse, undirected, unlimited accountability to the "public." Certainly in the case of persistent law violations, such measures are justified and quite likely authorized under existing law. In the case of generic industry problems, public directors and their companies would need to be exempted from antitrust liability if they were to consult with each other. Such consultation seems necessary since competition may make it difficult for one company to control its pollution unless others also do so. The use of such directors would thus have to be limited to cases in which a true social cost exists. If not, "unstable markets" might be considered a "generic problem" and public directors would become the vehicle for a price-fixing or market-dividing cartel.

Beyond Stone's limited approach, there is little value in confusing issues of corporate governance with issues of social control. These issues become hopelessly obscured when they are not carefully sep-

---

[24] Christopher D. Stone, "Public Directors Merit a Try," 54 Harv. Bus. Rev. 20 (1976).

arated. Assertions about shareholder protection are answered by charges of pollution, and only the world outlook of the speaker is made clear. If fruitful analysis is desired, a separation of these issues is necessary.

Corporate Power: The Bottom Line

Commissioner A. A. Sommer, Jr., was quoted at the beginning of this chapter on the power of corporations "to decide whether a plant will be closed, thus impoverishing a community; to . . . curtail production, thereby adding massively . . . to the rolls of the unemployed . . . to blunder and thereby harm the interests of those depending upon the prosperity of the enterprise for jobs."[25] This statement, typical of contemporary discussions of the modern corporation, strongly suggests that American corporations are too powerful and somehow must be brought under control. Others, in a similar vein, have analogized the problem of corporate power to the need for separation of powers in government.[26]

Consider Sommer's statement in detail, however. It is true that a corporation can close down a plant and injure the local economy. In virtually every case, however, either the plant is uneconomical (in the sense that consumers will not pay the true cost, including opportunity cost, of what the plant produces) or its functions can be performed more cheaply elsewhere, an opportunity the firm's competitors will quickly seize if it does not. The area of discretion consciously available to management, if any, is only to deal with the uncertainty over economic consequences, rather than to act on personal whim. Similarly, consumer demand, not the idiosyncratic behavior of management, is the cause of curtailments in production. In both cases, "corporate power" is exercised in response to consumer tastes.

In the case of corporate blunders, shareholders will surely suffer, as risk-taking investors always do when things go sour, but how many others will suffer sustained damage? If the only thing wrong with a firm is the quality of its management, management can be replaced and the firm can continue to operate. A firm which declines as a result of new technology, a change in consumer tastes, or the like is suffering not from a corporate blunder so much as from the workings of a competitive market.

As the alternative to corporate power, the critics offer govern-

---

[25] Sommer, "A Keynote Address."
[26] Note 6 above.

ment, which they seem to view as a Lilliputian. We have had enough experience with government decisions, however, to compare them with those of a firm, and the comparison is hardly favorable. Whereas corporate plant closings are a response to consumers, government decisions which damage or destroy local communities are often based solely on political clout or even the whim of one person. The opening or closing of domestic military bases is often determined by little more than whether senators from one state have more seniority or more strategic committee assignments than senators from another. In city after city, local neighborhoods have been destroyed on the order of a few people responsible for urban renewal decisions.[27] And one well-known biography states that highway development in New York uprooted thousands solely on the whim of one man, Robert Moses.[28] Whether one is concerned about accountability or centralized power, shifting corporate decision making to the government seems counterproductive.

A firm can create hardships by curtailing production, but the alternative is to continue to make goods for which consumers are unwilling to pay the true cost. When government makes analogous decisions, the impact can be brutal and for no better purpose than the protection of special interests. Rent control protects tenants from paying the true cost of the space they occupy and from the competition of others seeking housing. It also creates disincentives to invest which lead to abandonment, inadequate construction, and the destruction of municipal tax bases. Minimum-wage laws protect certain unionized workers from competition, but at the price of the unemployment of marginal workers, particularly the young and minorities.

So far as corporate blunders are concerned, how do they stack up against Pearl Harbor, Vietnam, the Great Depression (caused by the Federal Reserve Board), and the present plight of New York City? Although the market deters corporate blunders by penalizing them, the Lockheed loan suggests that government may simply bail out the inefficient.

Corporations are not perpetual-motion machines which, once started, operate according to an independent will of their own. They survive (unless the government is somehow involved) only by satisfying consumers; the more they do so, the more they prosper. It is said that market forces exercise only the most general constraint on

---

[27] Martin Anderson, *The Federal Bulldozer* (New York: McGraw-Hill, 1967).
[28] Robert A. Caro, *The Power Broker: Robert Moses and the Fall of New York* (New York: Random House, 1975), pp. 850–84.

modern corporations[29]—a proposition that finds no support whatsoever in either economic theory or corporate practice. In even the most extreme case, that of a corporation with an exclusive government franchise on a good prized by consumers, the cost of producing one more unit will at some point exceed the revenue obtained by its sale; at another point (probably nearby), the marginal cost of one more unit will be less than the marginal revenue. In the former case, further production would be at a loss; in the latter, the failure to continue production would also be at a loss in the sense that fewer profits would be made. Through trial and error, the firm will seek a price and output at which marginal cost and marginal revenue are equal. To be sure, the monopolist seeking such a price and output level will restrict output and misallocate resources, but in response to—not in disregard of—market forces.

Some critics seem to suggest that such a monopolist will not be overly concerned with consumer tastes since it is presumably able to sell whatever it pleases. Again, however, no self-respecting monopolist would behave in such a fashion. If consumers prefer yellow widgets to blue ones or widgets with safety features to plain ones, and if they will pay the true cost of such improvements, the monopolist ignores their tastes only at a financial cost. Even in the case of a clear monopoly, therefore, markets do constrain corporate behavior, although output is restricted and resources are misallocated.

If monopoly is the problem, the remedy is surely in the antitrust laws and not in tinkering with the mechanisms of corporate governance. Indeed, public or constituent directors would almost surely increase the danger of monopolistic behavior, the exact opposite of the results intended.

Evidence is accumulating to show that we routinely exaggerate the extent of monopolistic forces in the economy. Prior to the Organization of Petroleum Exporting Countries (OPEC), for example, many people believed the oil industry to be noncompetitive and, at least to the extent that government restricted certain imports, they had some justification. Yet when the OPEC cartel became effective, it quadrupled the price of oil, confirming that the previous price was near the competitive level.[30] More significantly, recent studies indicate that economic concentration (when achieved through internal

---

[29] Barber, *American Corporation*, pp. 22–30; Stone, *Where the Law Ends*, p. 88 ff.; and see Nader.

[30] Richard B. Mancke, "Oil's Spoils," 50 *Pub. Int.* 106 (1978).

growth) benefits consumers because it reflects superior efficiency.[31] If so, it is government intervention, not the acts of private firms, which is most likely to restrict output and misallocate resources.

The discretion frequently perceived in corporate decisions is an illusion that stems from two sources. First, no business can actually plot demand and cost curves; all must act in circumstances marked by varying degrees of uncertainty. Businessmen do have discretion in the sense that they face a range of choices, as do quarterbacks in football games and contestants on quiz shows. But just as a quarterback who calls the wrong play may see his team suffer a loss or hopeful contestants may see their hopes dashed by a wrong answer, a firm which makes a bad judgment will suffer financial consequences. Firms that make the most accurate decisions will prosper, and the pressures of competition will cause all others to copy them and seek even more accuracy. This pragmatic groping for the profit-maximizing product and price-output ratio may well appear as discretion, but it is discretion fettered by market rewards and penalties.

The second source of the illusion of corporate discretion is that most critics treat even accurate responses to consumer demand as misuse of corporate power when they disagree with the end result. It is better politics to appear to be forcing seat belts on "giant" auto companies than upon a populace which doesn't want to buckle up. Ideologically, much of consumerism lacks a solid theoretical base because it cannot explain why industry forgoes the profits it would make if consumers were willing to pay the cost of what industry is alleged to be willfully failing to provide.[32] Corporate discretion is less an observable phenomenon than a politically convenient myth.

Moreover, the vaunted power of the corporate Brobdingnagian relative to other institutions is a gross exaggeration. The power of

---

[31] Harold Demsetz, *The Market Concentration Doctrine* (Washington, D.C.: American Enterprise Institute, 1973). See also Yale Brozen, "The Antitrust Task Force Deconcentration Recommendation," *Journal of Law and Economics*, vol. 13 (2) (October 1970); Paul W. McCracken and Thomas Gale Moore, *Competition and Market Concentration in the American Economy* (Washington, D.C.: American Enterprise Institute, 1973); John S. McGee, *In Defense of Industrial Concentration* (New York: Praeger, 1971); Harvey J. Goldschmid and others, eds., *Industrial Concentration: The New Learning* (Boston: Little, Brown, 1974).

[32] "Mr. Nader is quite revealing when he says, 'economists for the most part have failed . . . to show how corporations . . . have been able to divert scarce resources to uses that have little human benefit or are positively harmful.' One might as well muse over the failure of scientists to explain why the earth is flat." Ralph K. Winter, Jr., *The Consumer Advocate versus the Consumer* (Washington, D.C.: American Enterprise Institute, 1972), p. 7.

government in our society hardly needs description, and the power of other private institutions seems ample relative to the corporation. Organized labor, which represents a declining fraction of the work force, certainly appears to do better on Capitol Hill than business. Its defeats, for example, are usually in proposals it makes which do not pass. Business, on the other hand, rarely makes a major legislative proposal without substantial support from groups like labor, as in the case of the Lockheed loan. In fact, the political victories of business are usually temporary defeats of antibusiness legislation. Charles Lindblom recently argued that business has disproportionate influence over government and, as a way of demonstrating that business favors the status quo, cited a study finding that 85 percent of business communications with government officials were in opposition to legislation.[33] Yet, since legislation can help business as easily as injure it, this defensiveness strongly suggests that business is under systematic and constant assault by powerful forces. How, indeed, could an Occupational Safety and Health Act be enacted by a government dominated by business?

When the power of the media is compared with that of the corporation, it cannot be seriously argued that the conscious influence on American life exerted by all the manufacturing corporations in the country is even remotely close to that exercised by a single television network. The idea that, say, the steel industry has greater "comprehensive economic-social-political power" than the Washington Post Co. (which includes *Newsweek*), or Time, Inc., or the Columbia Broadcasting Co., is simple nonsense. Schwartz alludes to the Vietnam war as an example of corporate influence, but the business community never embraced the war with fervor and was neither more nor less hawkish than any other group outside the universities. His quarrel with business may be over the fact that corporations responded to government bids for weapons and ammunition. A refusal to respond, however, would have been a conscious exercise of the very "economic-social-political power" he deplores. Compared with the conscious decision of network representatives on how to report the Vietnam war,[34] the acts of corporate manufacturing officers were neutral. Vietnam is not an isolated exception to Schwartz's generalization. Consider also the role of William Randolph Hearst in bringing

---

[33] Charles E. Lindblom, *Politics and Markets* (New York: Basic Books, 1977), pp. 170–200, 207.

[34] Edward J. Epstein, *Between Fact and Fiction* (New York: Random House, 1975), pp. 210–32.

on the Spanish-American War and that of Henry R. Luce in affecting American policy toward China.[35]

Firms are essentially reactive, even when they anticipate shifts in consumer tastes and technological improvements. To be sure, they attempt to affect consumer behavior through advertising, but their advertising must compete with that of all other firms and industries as well as with all other forms of persuasion. Attempts to induce purchases of gas-guzzling autos are challenged by ads for compact cars, trips to Miami, and savings accounts, and by the trumpeting of alternative life-styles in the media and popular literature. Business attempts to influence public opinion on matters other than consumption are sporadic and often hapless, since businessmen rarely represent a single point of view, are not well versed in theories of public policy, and are usually very defensive politically. As Robert Bork has said:

> It is instructive to meet the leaders of the major American corporations when they are out of the office, gathered together, and thinking about their position in the society. These are the people thought of by the general public and by the critics of the corporate system as bold, rapacious, cunning leaders, the Machiavellis of our society. There could hardly be a greater disparity between that image and the reality. . . . One finds many of them to be docile, apprehensive, defensive, and unsure of how to respond to sharp and unrelenting attacks.
>
> I remember a talk in which a prominent businessman [at that time also chairman of a prominent business organization reputed by corporate critics to be of vaunted power in Congress] said that he and his colleagues were concerned that the large American corporation does not possess legitimacy in the eyes of the rest of the society. He asked how they could alter their modes of corporate governance in particular, in order to be accepted into the society as legitimate members. . . . I recall having two reactions to his approach.
>
> The first was surprise at the triviality of the response suggested. . . . Fiddling with corporate governance for no better reason than to defuse hostility and head off punishing "reforms" is like tinkering with a leaky faucet in the hope of averting the Johnstown flood.
>
> My other reaction was surprise at the mood of defeat, of lowered morale, that suffuses meetings to discuss problems of this sort. It is as though a large fraction of the

---

[35] W. A. Swanberg, *Citizen Hearst* (New York: Scribner's, 1961); and W. A. Swanberg, *Luce and His Empire* (New York: Scribner's, 1972).

community of business leaders wants to make preemptive concessions, as if they meet not to plan a fight against a wrongheaded movement but to discuss how best to negotiate the terms of surrender.[36]

The role of the corporation in consciously influencing American life should be contrasted with that of the universities. Higher education also faces competition from ideas from sources outside the university —family, literature, experience, and so on. Still, the most—usually the only—sustained and systematic exposure of most persons to underlying issues of public policies is in the universities, and that exposure is heavily slanted by the political outlook of university faculties. As a student over twenty years ago, I heard jokes about the "two Republicans" in an economics department and the "only Republican" on a law faculty. Subsequently, as a faculty member, I was astonished to see the academic world consider as hard-core right wing a colleague who had campaigned for Robert F. Kennedy in 1968. Within the university community he *was* to the right, because most faculties are composed of persons who represent a small, very leftist segment of the universe of discourse. I would not expect or want universities to replicate the world of opinions precisely. Nevertheless, it seems evident that factors other than merit influence the selection of faculty, and the failure to present a reasonable diversity of viewpoint is accepted within the university community as not at all troubling but as proper.

Academic opinion on public issues is thus usually slanted in one direction. In academic discussions of corporate law the almost universal opinion among faculty members at every major law school is that more federal regulation is needed to protect shareholders because Delaware has led "a race for the bottom."[37] One searches in vain for an explanation of how Delaware can monopolize the market for capital and somehow force Saudi sheiks to pour their petrodollars into the greedy arms of Delaware management or why powerful institutional investors cannot find alternative investment opportunities that do not subject them to "sold" law. Instead, academic opinion follows herd-like after Cary, whose article offers no explanation of Delaware's supposed capture of international capital.[38]

In virtually every field, this narrow segment of opinion is openly antagonistic to the private sector and is relentlessly pressing for more

---

[36] Robert H. Bork, *Capitalism and the Corporate Executive* (Washington, D.C.: American Enterprise Institute, 1977), pp. 2–3.

[37] See chapter 2, note 6.

[38] See chapter 2, notes 8–14 and accompanying text.

and more government control. In economics, a social science with a theoretical content that might be supportive of capitalism, an outright defense of the private sector is known as the "Chicago School," a term which indicates how much of a curiosity this line of thought is in the mainstream of American academia.

This long-standing tilt in American higher education has inevitably affected public opinion and is one cause of the enormous growth of government over the last forty to fifty years. The political outlook of university faculties has shaped what Irving Kristol calls the New Class[39] of journalists, academics, polemicists, public interest advocates, and so on. This group, which has steadily grown in influence during this century, finds its power in the ability to influence government and regards the private or commercial sector as a threat to its own ascendancy.

Common observation suggests that forces supporting the private sector are today far more vulnerable politically than those pressing to diminish its role. The political party most closely associated with business in the public's mind is in great decline. President Carter showed no hesitation in delivering a blistering attack on the oil companies for opposing his energy plan, but he declined to criticize the media for helping to drive—quite unjustly, according to Mr. Carter's own view of the facts—his close friend and adviser, Bert Lance, from public life. The leading proponent of economic deconcentration in the United States Senate in recent years came from General Motors' home state, and the steady legislative trend has been antibusiness. The increasing power of politically active nonbusiness groups addressing environmental issues, product regulation, minority demands, feminist proposals, political reform, health programs, and so on, hardly supports the claim that corporations dominate our life.

There are two reasons why the myth of corporate dominance persists. First, it is politically convenient to have a group to blame for society's ills and to divert attention from the weaknesses of one's own programs. This is a familiar ploy in all societies and appears in a variety of forms, ranging from virulent racism to well-meant calls for less materialism. Almost invariably, the target labeled as a grave threat to the political system is rarely able even to defend itself. If it had the power to retaliate effectively, in fact, it would not have been chosen to play the role of scapegoat.

The use of the corporation for these purposes has become almost an American tradition. As Huey Long, one who knew, said, "Corpo-

---

[39] Irving Kristol, "Corporate Capitalism in America," 41 *Pub. Int.* 124, 133–35 (1975).

rations are the finest political enemies in the world."[40] The perception that one's cause will be furthered if somehow it can be transformed into an attack on business is a notorious political fact. Thus, business is attacked for the Vietnam war, which had far stronger roots in academia; "giant" auto companies are charged with depriving purchasers of seat belts, when all evidence indicates a lack of interest among the driving public; and the fuss over shareholder protection is supported only by those who are palpably disinterested in corporate success. Such phenomena could appear only in a society in which corporate influence is in steady decline and an anticorporate posture pays political dividends.

A second reason for the persistence of the myth of corporate dominance stems from confusing commercial size with power. Corporate assets or sales statistics may be astronomical, to be sure, but neither the possession of resources nor a high level of business activity necessarily implies great political or even "comprehensive economic-social-political power." Consider a simple example. A general store in a rural area may conduct most of the retail business in that area, its fixtures and land may give it a large asset value relative to other businesses, and statistics might be culled which make its commercial dominance seem self-evident. The term "monopoly," as commonly used by corporate critics, would apply to the store; indeed, one could argue rhetorically that the people of the area are wholly dependent upon it for the necessities of life. From none of this would it follow that the store or its owner has dominant influence in the town, even though retailing skills in such circumstances might well overlap with political skills. Complaints of high prices, lack of credit, and other exercises of "discretion" might abound, whether the owner prospers or is on the margin.

Corporations are conduits of exchange between consumers and a variety of factors of production, such as labor and capital. Because it serves as the principal crossroad, so to speak, at which these factors intersect, the corporate function assumes the superficial appearance of "comprehensive economic-social-political power." Because it is a conduit, however, it is not a static repository of resources available for the wielding of societal power. At best a corporation has (some) money available for advertising about public issues, the least efficient means of shaping public opinion.

None of this is to argue that the media or the universities or whatever ought to have their power reduced by government. Even

---

[40] T. Harry Williams, *Huey Long* (New York: Knopf, 1969), p. 416.

less is it an argument that corporations should have dominance. On the contrary, a private sector that neither controls, nor is controlled by, government is essential to freedom. The point is that gross exaggerations of corporate power are being employed by those who want to bring about centralization of power in government or who are working to this end in ignorance of the consequences of their acts. The intrusion of government into corporate management will not only increase the quantum of government power but also significantly politicize what are now private market decisions. The exercise of managerial discretion in response to market demands is a decentralized process with ultimate authority resting in consumers. Once the conscious hand of government is introduced into the exercise of managerial authority, that authority will be relocated and centralized. Consumers will no longer be able to bid to satisfy their tastes, and market decisions will be increasingly influenced by the demands of organized economic interest groups and the desire to reward political friends and punish political enemies. Massive raw political power will have been created and centralized. At that point, the mythical corporate Brobdingnagian will become fact as a result of the very measures supposed to cut it down to size. To bring about this result in the name of our constitutional separation of powers is like justifying Idi Amin's regime on First Amendment grounds.

4

Summary and Conclusion

Two conflicting views of the relation of the corporation to government have struggled for dominance ever since the corporate form came into being. One views incorporation as a special privilege, the exercise of which must be carefully monitored and regulated by government. The other treats the corporate form as a species of contract which is no more subject to government regulation than other contracts between private parties. "Enabling" state corporation codes are based on the latter view. Calls for federal incorporation or other federal legislation limiting managerial discretion and designed to regulate the corporation's relation to shareholders or to society reflect the former view.

The claim that federal legislation is necessary to protect shareholders is based on the conventional wisdom that the competition between states for corporate charters works to the disadvantage of shareholders. That proposition, however, is on its face implausible. Corporations must attract capital from a vast range of competing opportunities, and the state that rigs its code to benefit management unfairly will drive debt and equity capital away. Much of the criticism of the Delaware code, moreover, rests on the assumption that greater regulation of corporate transactions will not impose costs as well as benefits on shareholders.

The costs and benefits of such regulation can be determined only after identifying the market functions of, and market constraints on, corporate management. If management is not successful in product-market competition or if it does not assure shareholders of a competitive return on their investment, the price of the firm's stock will drop. This drop will facilitate a takeover by parties seeking a capital gain (or increased management compensation) by replacing the old management with more efficient personnel. This market for management control thus disciplines corporate management.

It has been argued, however, that imperfections in the form of high takeover costs seriously lessen the effect of this market constraint. High takeover costs which result from state and federal law or from management efficiency either demonstrate a need for less regulation or reflect the fact that shareholders are protected. Nevertheless, transaction costs in the market for management control—particularly information costs—may be quite high.

It is very difficult, however, to limit the discretion of corporate management without impairing corporate efficiency. The economic theory of the firm strongly suggests that the management function will best be performed by persons who receive a share of residual profits. Management's discretion in rewarding itself is such an entitlement, and there is strong reason to believe that increases in management's discretion will be accompanied by increases in shareholder benefit. Shareholder vulnerability lies in the chance that management may be indifferent to the long run and seek a one-shot gain by looting or otherwise permanently impairing the corporation.

State corporation codes seem quite consistent with this theory of the corporation in that they permit management discretion but impose limits on transactions that may raid corporate assets. One would expect competitive state legal systems to tend toward economically optimal rules governing the corporation-shareholder relation because of competition in the capital market. The liberality of state law is thus evidence, not of management overreaching, but of state law's moving in a direction consistent with an economic model of the management function.

Takeover statutes differ, however, since, unlike rules governing management conflict of interest and so on, they regulate the market for management control rather than the capital market. In the market for management control, monopolization by state law may be possible because existing management has little incentive to seek out optimal arrangements and states must fear reincorporation. More important, takeover statutes are extraterritorial in effect. Here the competition for charters is actually of little effect since such takeover legislation overrides the corporation code of the chartering state. The recent wave of takeover statutes is evidence of a need for federal regulation to protect competition in that market.

The claim that federal regulation of internal corporate governance is necessary in the interest of certain social goals rests on a number of general and undifferentiated concerns about the "comprehensive economic-social-political power" of corporations. Among the remedies designed to check this power are proposals mandating the representation of affected groups in corporate decision making. If representatives of labor, commercial consumers, final consumers, suppliers, and the public are placed on corporate boards, the much-decried "separation of ownership and control" would become a complete break. Not only is it unlikely that such constituent directors would be bound by a fiduciary duty to shareholders, but it is also quite likely that management would find it in its interest to bargain for quid pro quos with such directors and form an alliance against shareholders. Furthermore, such representation necessarily involves conversations between horizontal competitors about trading terms and would necessitate repeal of the Sherman Act. The model for constituent directors is thus not democracy or the separation of powers but Italian fascism and the National Recovery Administration.

No criteria are suggested to govern the conduct of public directors —other than the usual political pressures of powerful groups. Nor do the critics' proposals describe how other groups to be represented should be identified or defined and their representatives selected. The failure to address such issues casts doubt on the seriousness of the proposals. Were they enacted into law, they would surely impair the ability of corporations to raise capital. Government might feel obliged to intervene more frequently than ever before to prevent corporate bankruptcies.

Calls for the wholesale disclosure of corporate information ignore the very high costs such measures would impose on the price of doing business, unavoidable costs which would ultimately have to be borne by consumers. The benefits of disclosure, however, seem sporadic, particularly since only a fraction of the mountain of paper produced would be read, and disclosure would probably be a heavier burden on small firms than on large. Disclosure should thus be limited to cases in which it is necessary to enforce government policy or where an appropriate agency or committee desires the information to evaluate a new policy.

Some critics have called for the federal chartering of corporations so as to provide remedies for the violation of such regulatory statutes as the antitrust laws. The only remedy chartering would provide that is not available at present, however, is a prohibition on the right to do business. But that would adversely affect suppliers, customers, and employees as well and is so Draconian that it would probably never be used. There has been no demonstration, moreover, that the normal remedies for violations of the law are insufficient. One suggestion by Christopher Stone is worth considering: judical appointment of a public director for a limited time and purpose where repeated corporate delinquency has been demonstrated or where a generic problem exists in an industry.

The assertions about corporate dominance of our society that support such proposals are gross exaggerations. Many of the acts attributed to corporate power are little more than responses to consumer behavior or to changes in the cost of doing business. Unlike government policies, very few major corporate decisions are matters of personal whim. Corporate mistakes rarely are as brutal and destructive as those of government.

Other institutions in the society, such as the media and the universities, have more influence on public opinion than the corporation and exercise it more deliberately. The steady shrinkage of the private sector over recent years suggests, not that corporations exercise overweening power, but that they are in headlong retreat. Indeed, the drumfire of criticism directed at them can be explained only by weakness, not strength, and by the truth of Huey Long's dictum, "Corporations are the finest political enemies in the world."

The American corporation is a remarkably successful device for raising large amounts of capital and for mixing that capital with a complex of other factor inputs. Because the productivity of other inputs is correspondingly increased and economies of scale reduce costs to consumers, all groups in the society have benefited from corporate activity. These quite beneficial events have taken place in the absence of the regulation of corporate governance. In fact, they took place after the corporate form ceased to be a specially granted privilege. It was the movement from the state-granted privilege of "special" incorporation to "enabling" corporation codes as a species of contract law that permitted private parties to seek out the most efficient means of doing business and competing freely. Regulation was important to this very beneficial turn of events only in its disappearance. Critical to the process was the competition between states for corporate charters because investors and management were enabled to seek out the best available legal systems. And the legal systems themselves were thereby induced to evolve in a way consistent with the underlying economic functions of the resulting business units.

The call for federal intervention is a call to move away from this view of corporate charters as a species of contract and to move toward the older and justifiably rejected view of charters as a species of government privilege. Although the movement parades under the